"If you l ....ow
he deliv........................., ..u practical recourses for
everyday leaders like you and me. **In his book *UNREA-
SONABLE CHURCHES*, Rich keeps true to his track
record by providing real examples of innovative
ideas that work in local churches along with the
encouragement to help you know you can do it too!**
It's an insider's look into some of the best practices to
help any church reach its full potential."

— **DAN REILAND, EXECUTIVE PASTOR, 12STONE® CHURCH**

"Many times we try to put God in a box to figure out how
He grows churches and forms ministry strategies, but
the reality is that God cannot be contained. He works
uniquely in each church and in each community, and I am
thrilled that **Rich has captured these insightful stories of brave church leaders who have followed God's
promptings and seen incredible results.**"

— **HEATHER LARSON, EXECUTIVE PASTOR, WILLOW CREEK
COMMUNITY CHURCH**

"Rich has an incredible gift for bringing practical insight
and wisdom to the churches' most unique and often overwhelming challenges. *UNREASONABLE CHURCHES* is a
**great resource to take your next steps in improving
your ministry.**"

— **FRANK BEALER, FAMILY PASTOR, ELEVATION CHURCH**

"One thing I've learned in two decades of church leadership is that many leaders would rather make excuses than make progress. The truth is, you can make excuses or you can make progress but you can't make both.

If you want to keep making excuses, don't read this book.

If you want to make progress, prepare to become unreasonable."

—CAREY NIEUWHOF, FOUNDING AND TEACHING PASTOR, CONNEXUS CHURCH, WWW.CAREYNIEUWHOF.COM

"*UNREASONABLE CHURCHES* challenges church leaders to think daringly about 'the way things have always been done.' **Rich challenges the Church to take risks on trying new approaches to ministry including giving leadership training, follow up, and more.** The case studies of churches innovating and reaching uncharted territory, along with takeaway questions, are inspiring and worth every penny spent on the book!"

—TIM STEVENS, VANDERBLOEMEN SEARCH GROUP

"**Rich has done the church an epic favor by writing this book.** He's a master storyteller, and he knows what he's talking about! I'm excited for you to read this valuable resource."

—DERWIN L. GRAY, LEAD PASTOR TRANSFORMATION CHURCH, AUTHOR OF *THE HIGH DEFINITION LEADER: LEADING MULTIETHNIC CHURCHES IN A MULTIETHNIC WORLD*

"Having served as an executive pastor for nearly 12 years, I understand the temptation to mimic the success of other churches. **In *UNREASONABLE CHURCHES*, Rich has gathered an inspiring collection of stories about leaders who are passionately pursuing the ministry God has for their church. It's an important reminder that each call is unique and radically different.** I know you'll be encouraged to seek God for a better understanding of the influence of your church."

—JENNI CATRON, FOUNDER OF THE 4SIGHT GROUP AND AUTHOR OF *THE 4 DIMENSIONS OF EXTRAORDINARY LEADERSHIP*

"A tremendously giant part of leading is knowing when and how to take risks, knowing how to hear God's voice telling you when it's time to "zig when others zag" as Rich Birch puts it. **Rich's experience in church and ministry, coupled with his great passion to see people put their hope in Jesus, make his voice one that I believe should be heard, especially on the topic of making an impact on the world.**"

—DINO RIZZO, EXECUTIVE DIRECTOR AT ASSOCIATION OF RELATED CHURCHES, ASSOCIATE PASTOR AT CHURCH OF THE HIGHLANDS

"When it comes to loving and equipping the local church, I do not know anyone doing a better job than Rich Birch! Rich takes his passion and not only learns for himself but shares what he has learned in an attempt to make everyone better! *UNREASONABLE CHURCHES* will be a huge tool for every pastor and leader to be better at what God has called them to do!"

"Rich has a way of going beneath the surface and revealing the heart of what makes a church tick. **In *UNREASONABLE CHURCHES*, Rich shows you how the Church will look in the future and what you can learn from those who are already there.**"

"***UNREASONABLE CHURCHES* tells 10 compelling stories that show how crazy steps of faith are really the most logical way for church leaders to live and lead.** Rich Birch has a rare ability to find those 'out of the box' insights that help ministry leaders make breakthroughs in their thinking and strategy. Inspiring. Accessible. Practical. And completely unreasonable."

"It can be overwhelming with so many church resources to choose from in our generation. **This book is a MUST have. The stories of what God is doing in the Church are inspiring. The practical applications are refreshing.** You actually feel like you can apply this book to your life and ministry! **Rich Birch hit a grand slam with this one.**"

"Church help and resources that exist today can be full of theories and "ideas", but **Rich has been offering church leaders practical help that goes beyond theory and dives in to the guts 'how-to get it done.'**"

—BOBBY WILLIAMS, LEAD PASTOR, RIDGE CHURCH

"I love how this book presents ten most **wonderful stories of innovative churches stepping out by faith beyond reason to do something unprecedented that's yielding fruitfulness for the Kingdom of God!** I don't know about you, but I find these examples of real-life stories to be far more inspiring than a bunch of pithy quotes any day."

—DJ CHUANG, STRATEGY CONSULTANT AND AUTHOR OF
MULTIASIAN.CHURCH

"If you're looking for a trusted friend who's been around the block and knows his stuff, then Rich is your man. His book, ***UNREASONABLE CHURCHES***, **is a helpful guide for any church leader wanting to cut right to the heart of the most effective ministry models and trends.** His breadth of knowledge is matched by the depths of his insights and **this resource will leave you inspired, provoked and excited to lead in your context.**"

—CHRISTA HESSELINK, SPEAKER AND AUTHOR OF *LIFE'S GREAT
DARE: RISKING IT ALL FOR THE ABUNDANT LIFE*

"If you are looking for the things they don't teach you in Bible College, look no further! **Rich has an uncanny**

ability to bring clarity to how, when, why, and what we should be doing in the church. I highly recommend this book to anyone who is in or about to be in ministry."

—DOUGLAS J GARASIC, AUTHOR OF *NOTORIOUS*, PASTOR OF THE
MOVEMENT

"I don't know of anyone more in-tune with what's working currently in church leadership than Rich Birch. Rich provides helpful insights for church leaders to consider when navigating the demands of leading a church. I'm a fan of outside-the-box thinking, maybe even unreasonable thinking, this is why **I LOVE how Rich digs into churches that decided to do things differently, take some risks, and see a greater impact.** If you're involved in leading a church in any capacity, you will benefit from this book! I highly recommend it."

—LANE SEBRING, AUTHOR OF *PREACHING KILLER SERMONS*,
MINISTRY BLOGGER AT PREACHINGDONKEY.COM

"Thinking of doing something different? Check out *UNREASONABLE CHURCHES*. Rich Birch brings together inspiring stories from several churches. They're getting results by doing things in a way others aren't. What's more, **Rich provides practical takeaways that will help your church navigate through our changing times. Every church leader who wants to stay relevant should read this book.**"

—ROB CIZEK, EXECUTIVE PASTOR, NORTHSHORE CHRISTIAN
CHURCH, WWW.ROBCIZEK.COM

"Rich Birch's *UNREASONABLE CHURCHES* is delivered in typical Rich Birch style—**inspirational and practical. Each church is highlighted in a way that any church can connect to, regardless of geography, theology, or size.** My favorite book feature is "takeaway points to act on," where Rich offers 5-plus ideas of practical next steps at the end of each chapter."

—GREGG FARAH, LEAD PASTOR, SHELTER ROCK CHURCH – WESTBURY, ASSOCIATE AT THE SLINGSHOT GROUP

"Too many churches today are looking for the reasonable answer—a fair and sensible way to expand the Kingdom safely. **Rich's charge to be "unreasonable" in your approach to ministry is inspiring yet incredibly challenging. Each section leads the reader to consider where they are in ministry and the "unreasonable" steps to consider in getting where they never believed they could**... to a new, inspirational approach of impacting the world through the local church.

—DR. JOSH WHITEHEAD, EXECUTIVE PASTOR, FAITH PROMISE CHURCH

"I got the chance to get to know Rich Birch and the unSeminary team this year and was blown away by their passion to help pastors learn everything they wished they had learned in seminary. **Their devotion to practical, helpful, and insightful leadership teaching was refreshing. In his book *UNREASONABLE CHURCHES*, Rich continues in this same vein.** The book shares real life stories from a variety of churches and pulls out phe-nomenally practical leadership insights for the pastors of today! This is a must read!"

"**Rich Birch's latest book, *UNREASONABLE CHURCHES*, is a gift to the Church.** Rich's love for people and the local church is evident through his passion and insights. His desire to help local churches grow and develop people is communicated through clear and practical teaching. Put these into practice and watch God work in your church."

"I've had the pleasure of knowing Rich for many years, and the impact of his work has gone well beyond the walls of his own church. From multisite operations to staff tran-sitions to special projects, Rich is one of the first guys I contact when I've got an idea I want to explore.

"**Readers will find practical, inspiration, helpful infor-mation in this new book and can trust that Rich has gone ahead and done so much of the work for you.** I'm grateful to Rich, for this book and for how God is empow-ering His church to reach people for Jesus in new ways."

"Rich Birch, his leadership, his podcast, and his coaching have made a difference in numerous churches over the years, and **I'm so glad he's sharing these stories in the book and giving us permission to dream again and then take action. Get multiple copies of this for your team and discuss it with them.**"

—GREG ATKINSON, AUTHOR, LEADERSHIP COACH AND CONSULTANT

"These are ten engaging stories packed with ridiculously insightful and inspiring thoughts from churches and leaders around the country—ones I wish I could sit and have coffee with. **This book is a game changing resource rich with wisdom and thoughtful challenges that will impact my thinking and approach to ministry without a doubt!**"

—SONJA WALTMAN, EXECUTIVE DIRECTOR OF MINISTRIES, LCBC CHURCH

"Brace yourself... *UNREASONABLE CHURCHES* will challenge the mundane and status quo and revolutionize the way you think about church growth. Filled with inspiring stories and powerful and practical, thought-provoking questions, *UNREASONABLE CHURCHES* serves as the catalyst we all need to shake up the way we 'do' church. **If you're comfortable and satisfied with what you've got, put this book down. But if you're serious about reaching the lost, then by all means, read on and get ready to STOP playing it safe and START changing the world!**"

—CHRISTINE KREISHER, DISCIPLESHIP PASTOR AT GT CHURCH AND AUTHOR OF *THE VOLUNTEER PROJECT: STOP RECRUITING. START RETAINING.*

"In talking about the high challenge of following Christ, Rich Birch shares real-life examples of courageous people and churches. But this isn't enough! How do we bring home these principles? At the end of each chapter, Rich gives both: questions to consider and takeaway points to act on. This makes the book **a great read of both ideas and principles to apply.**"

—DAVID FLETCHER, EXECUTIVE PASTOR, EVFREE FULLERTON, FOUNDER OF XPASTOR.ORG

10 CHURCHES WHO **ZAGGED** WHEN OTHERS **ZIGGED**...
AND SAW MORE **IMPACT** BECAUSE OF IT!

UN**REASONABLE**
CHURCHES

RICH BIRCH
FOREWORD BY CAREY NIEUWHOF

To all the **CHURCH LEADERS** wondering if you can, this book is permission.

To the **LEADERS** who trusted me when I was young... that was an unreasonable move.

To my **AMAZING WIFE** for putting up with all these years of unreasonableness.

Table of Contents

CAREY NIEUWHOF

THIS IS A BIT OF A DANGEROUS BOOK.

SOMETIMES AS CHURCH leaders, we talk ourselves out of progress by offering a series of excuses and justifications that leave us exactly where we are—stuck.

We can't change because:

It's too expensive

That will never work here

Our denomination won't let us

People won't accept it

The idea is too radical

And when you look around, you probably feel you're justified in feeling that way because frankly, nobody else is taking the risks required to make progress either.

That's why *UNREASONABLE CHURCHES* is a dangerous book. Rich simply takes away all your excuses. Rich doesn't just write theory. He profiles 10 actual churches who took real risks few were willing to take, and who made progress in their mission because of it.

If you look at the profile of churches that make an impact, that's always what happens. In my two decades of leadership, most of what we did seemed unreasonable.

17

I started ministry in three small churches that everyone had written off as dead. None of the churches had grown in 40 years. There was only one problem: God hadn't written off those churches or their people. When we introduced a new vision and a driving desire to reach young families, the churches started to grow. Unreasonable, but it worked!

We grew fast enough that we sold all three historic buildings and united our ministries by starting a new church with a new name on a new site with a new mission. Unreasonable, but it worked!

Then we embarked on a multi-million dollar building project trying to reach more people; unreasonable for churches that had a combined budget of $45,000 just a few years earlier, but it worked!

Then, we wondered if we could reach more unchurched people if we restarted in a non-denominational context, so we walked away from a nearly paid-for building and started over again as Connexus Church—a portable church in two nearby cities hoping to reach more people. Unreasonable, but it worked because now 60% of all people who come to Connexus self-identify as having no regular church attendance pattern. Rich knows this part of the story personally, as well, because he helped us make that move when we had the privilege of being on staff together.

We were then told we would never be able to build in one of the cities because of cost, zoning, and a city that wouldn't change by-laws. So we prayed and gently lobbied City Hall for several years until the city not only changed the zoning for us, but for all churches across the city. And then we moved into a new permanent broadcast campus. Unreasonable, but it worked.

The difference between churches that make an impact and churches that don't is this: leaders who are willing to be unreasonable.

In classic Rich-form, Rich has found the outliers who break rules, challenge assumptions and actually move the mission forward. The biggest surprise? They're leaders just like you and me who lead churches just like yours and mine. Most aren't even famous. They're just effective.

One thing I've learned in two decades of church leadership is that many leaders would rather make excuses than make progress. The truth is, you can make excuses or you can make progress, but you can't make both.

If you want to keep making excuses, don't read this book.

If you want to make progress, prepare to become unreasonable.

– Carey Nieuwhof
Founding and Teaching Pastor, Connexus Church
www.careynieuwhof.com

Introduction:
IT'S TIME TO GET UNREASONABLE

I CAN STILL REMEMBER it like it was yesterday. There I was, nearly 20 years ago, sitting in the third row at the lakeside auditorium of Willow Creek Community Church with tears in my eyes. It felt like the first time I was experiencing a church that was making a difference to its community. I was relatively new in ministry and had heard about this crazy church in the suburbs of Chicago that was trying ministry in a new manner. They had centered their ministry around the novel idea that they should talk about stuff that people are interested in and use that as a bridge to the gospel of Jesus. It was a radical idea then and is still revolutionizing churches today.

But why was I crying watching them do ministry? What was it about this community of Christ followers reaching out to their city in this manner that moved me that deeply? How was it that a church just being the church was such a moving thing to watch? Did I have something weird to eat at the food court before the service, or was there something deeper going on?

Reflecting on it now, I believe what was moving me was the deep sense that this group of people was going against the flow to try something radical in the name of Jesus to make a difference. At some deep level, I was connecting with all the pain this leadership had gone through to make this amazing thing happen, and it moved me at my core. What started in me that day was a desire to learn from churches that were eager to try new tactics for the sake of impacting their communities, for the sake of the gospel. I was moved by the leadership community at Willow Creek during that service I attended because of the choices they had made to reach people, and I'm still moved today by leaders of all kinds of churches who make similar decisions.

I think churches that make "against the flow" decisions to create an impact in their communities are being unreasonable, and I love it! Unreasonable because they refuse to play it safe, choosing instead to take risks that other churches are frankly too cowardly to make. 94% of all churches are losing ground against the growth of the communities they serve.[1] Stop for a minute and think about this fact. The vast majority of churches in North America is losing influence and has diminished impact. Now is the time for us to look for churches that are acting "unreasonable" and having increasing impact and influence because of it. In fact, in a time when the vast majority of churches are plateaued or in decline, the only reasonable thing to do is to look to the unreasonable fringe where God is using leaders who aren't afraid to try something different. In a day and age where the light of the church has faded

1 http://www.churchleaders.com/pastors/pastor-articles/139575-7-star-tling-facts-an-up-close-look-at-church-attendance-in-america.html

to a faint flicker, we need to find centers of unreasonable innovation where the light is burning bright.

I'm fanboy of the local church and especially local church leaders. I'm moved by leaders who are looking to make a difference in their communities through the local church. I love hearing the stories of local church leaders who have tried something new and it's worked. This book is a celebration of innovation and guts in the local church. All the leaders you're going to meet in these pages have faced obstacles and yet seen the reward of having an impact in their communities. You're going to get a chance to learn from leaders you probably haven't heard of before, and I hope you'll be moved to try something unreasonable at your church. Don't imitate what they have done, rather pursue a path of innovation and try something totally new.

We need you and your church to be unreasonable. If we all just keep following what has always been done in other churches, we will continue to see the decreasing impact. If we look only to what we've learned in seminary and pattern our ministries after that, we garner the results that we're seeing around us—weak and irrelevant churches. We need to push through our fears to see a brand new impact—God wants to do something new in our day. I really do believe the best is yet to come in the local church and rather than seeing a few models repeated and replicated in a homogenous manner, we need a variety of fresh approaches to meet the realities we're facing today. My hope is that this book serves as permission for you to dream a new dream and start taking action toward what you believe God wants to do in your community!

In the coming pages you're going to read about modern day heroes of the faith who made crazy decisions for the sake of the gospel. Rather than just doing what was expected of them, each individual made a God-inspired choice to take a leap of faith in the ministry they served. Here are a few snapshots of the churches you'll hear about:

- A dwindling 192-year-old church that, rather than closing its doors, gave up all its assets to a young church plant to help fuel its mission. The sacrifice of the seniors still in attendance results in exponential impact on the next generation.

- A church that opens its doors throughout the week to its community. Rather than just doing church on Sunday, this church is practically serving its community 7 days a week and seeing huge fruit from it!

- Two churches that are working to serve the "cast members" of Walt Disney World in Florida with ministry models uniquely designed to cater to this community of 74,000 people!

- A church that has rejected the traditional "segregated" constructs of most evangelical churches and is thriving at building a multicultural community of Christ followers on a mission to make a difference in their city and beyond!

- A church that launched five new campuses on one Sunday because they were convicted that they had become too comfortable in their approach to ministry!

As you read the stories of these churches, I ask you to resist the urge to think that your church couldn't attempt these radical innovations. I've interacted with every one of these churches and they are just normal people like you and me. They aren't superhuman nor have any special level of revelation from Jesus to lead. They are church leaders like you who are gripped by what God might do in their community and have had the guts to take action. Marinate in these stories and ask Jesus what unreasonable next steps he would have you take in your church. Use these examples to move you and your team to think about something new for your community. Don't attempt to duplicate what these leaders did, but allow the spirit of what they attempted to push you to ask big questions. In order to have the impact that your church needs to have, you are going to have to try something that no one else has tried.

Are you ready to be unreasonable?

Chapter 1:

UNREASONABLE
FUNDRAISING

THREE BOYS WERE bragging about their dads, trying to one-up each other with the best "my dad makes more money than your dad" story. The first boy said proudly, "My dad is a doctor. He talks to people for 30 minutes and gets $500." Not to be outdone, the second boy boasted, "Oh yeah? My dad's a lawyer. He talks to people for 30 minutes and gets $1,000." The third boy said, "I can top that easy. My dad's a preacher. He talks to people for 30 minutes and it takes 16 guys to collect all the money!"

Raising money for your church can be one of the most difficult and misunderstood things church leaders do. Both skeptics and church budget-nazis scoff when the preacher asks a congregation to dig deep and cough it up. Church leaders are trained to be disciple-makers, not fundraisers. It's hard enough to go through a major capital campaign *once* in the life of a church, but it's *unreasonable* to do a million dollar fundraiser *twice*, within *six months*. Sounds impossible? It probably is, but Elevate Life Church did it.

PART OF SOMETHING GREATER

No matter what a church and its leaders plan, God—not donors—is the ultimate source of everything!

Levi was one of Jacob's twelve sons to whom a portion of real estate was allotted in the Promised Land, through Abraham; however, in the list of the tribes who eventually *received* land, Levi's name was not listed! Why? Levi's portion was given to one of Joseph's sons, but in place of the land, God promised Levi and his offspring tithes and offerings.

Levi's descendants were born into this position—one tribe, chosen to serve the other eleven by administrating and tending to the duties of the Tabernacle (and later, the Temple).

The Israelites understood this tithe to be an offering to the Lord, as revealed in the Old Testament:

> For the tithe of the sons of Israel, which they offer as an offering *to the LORD*, I have given to the Levites.
> – NUMBERS 18:24, EMPHASIS ADDED

The lamb or sheave of grain an Israelite offered to the Levites was not a horizontal gift from an Israelite to a Levite but rather a vertical gift from an Israelite *to his God.* It may seem like giving is a horizontal act, from a person to a church for example, but when it is in response to a person's love for the Lord, and out of obedience to Him, it is vertical. It is a gift back to God, and the more people begin to see God as the source of everything to begin with, the more they will be moved to give generously with abandon—knowing it is going right back to the Giver!

After being freed from slavery from Egypt, Moses went before the whole Israelite community and said it was time to give an offering to the Lord. This offering was to be what would provide materials to build the Tabernacle, which would house the presence of the Lord! Notice people's response:

> Then the whole Israelite community withdrew from Moses' presence, and *everyone who was willing and whose heart moved them came* and brought an offering to the Lord for the work on the tent of meeting, for all its service, and for the sacred garments. All who were willing, men and women alike, came and brought gold jewelry of all kinds: brooches, earrings, rings, and ornaments. They all presented their gold as a wave offering to the Lord. Everyone who had blue, purple, or scarlet yarn, or fine linen, or goat hair, ram skins dyed red or other durable leather brought them. Those presenting an offering of silver or bronze brought it as an offering to the Lord, and everyone who had acacia wood for any part of the work brought it. Every skilled woman spun with her hands and brought what she had spun— blue, purple or scarlet yarn or fine linen. And all the women who were willing and had the skill spun the goat hair. The leaders brought

onyx stones and other gems to be mounted on the ephod and breastpiece. They also brought spices and olive oil for the light and for the anointing oil and for the fragrant incense. *All the Israelite men and women who were willing brought to the Lord freewill offerings for all the work the Lord* through Moses had commanded them to do.

– EXODUS 35:20–29, EMPHASIS ADDED

The offerings would go toward the construction of the Tabernacle, but Scripture is clear that the offerings ultimately were given to God. It probably seemed like a daunting task, but Scripture says God's people gave generously—and the Tabernacle was built, exactly to God's specifications as *"everyone who was willing and whose heart moved them came and brought an offering to the Lord for the work of the Tent of Meeting . . . "*

Deep inside their souls, people find joy in being a part of something that is significant and bigger than themselves. We see this clearly in the case of Elevate Life Church.

ELEVATE LIFE WAS BORN— AND GREW QUICKLY

With the help of the Association of Related Churches (ARC), Lead Pastor Tim Staier, his wife, and 15 others planted Elevate Life Church in the Oakleaf area of Jacksonville, Florida. The first Sunday in October 2010 saw 200 people in attendance at the high school cafeteria where they began meeting. In just a few years, the congregation included over 600 each Sunday at two campuses, one at the high school in Oakleaf and the other in a Fleming Island movie theater.

In 2014, Elevate Life was told they needed to make determined efforts to look elsewhere for a meeting place. They received a deadline; there would be no more meeting at the local high school cafeteria. They complied, looking around the Oakleaf area to discover available options. In their search, they found no viable option for leasing or purchasing in the Oakleaf area, so they returned to the school and asked if there was any way they could continue to meet in the school. The church leadership felt that staying around Oakleaf was essential to their ongoing ministry. The school gave Elevate Life an ultimatum: continuing to meet in the cafeteria was contingent on the church purchasing land as a building site.

At this point, many churches would be tempted to look in different neighborhoods for other leasing options. The prices in Oakleaf were high, the church had no extra resources, and they were a new church plant. Tim and the leaders of this unreasonable church were convinced that the continuing life of the church was dependent on keeping it at home, the neighborhood where Elevate Life had grown up. So the church agreed to the school's conditions and set out to find a piece of property. They also had to consider how they would fund the purchase. Land in Oakleaf is expensive, and they estimated that their church, which had an annual budget of $800,000, would need to raise $1,200,000 that year to be able to purchase the property.

NO LIMITS

They decided to take the need to 600 church members by presenting it in 60 small group meetings. Along with Executive Pastor Mark Mellen, Pastor Tim met with two groups every evening for six weeks. The leaders called the church members to work together and pledge the needed money over the next year. They called the campaign *No Limits*.

In the meetings, Pastor Tim showed a video which explained the church's urgent need to purchase land in order to continue meeting in Oakleaf. He then shared his vision for what the church could do and be in the community, finally inviting the small group members to share their stories about what Elevate Life meant to them. Many in the groups shared with full hearts and tears. After the sharing time, people were encouraged to consider joining the initiative. They were asked to pledge toward the annual budget and the needed funds to purchase land.

Following the small group meetings, the congregation gathered together for a Sunday night worship service, to make donation commitments and to receive an offering toward the land purchase. That evening, $1,200,000 was pledged for the year, and church members gave $500,000 toward their commitments. In one night, they had received almost half of the total and over half of the previous year's annual budget. They were able to purchase 25 acres of prime property in the Oakleaf area for $900,000.

RUN FOR ONE

But Elevate Life was not done with fundraising. The first campaign was born out of an urgent need. Six months down the road, they did the unthinkable and the unreasonable—they launched a *second* capital campaign, born out of a desire to expand their reach with the gospel. Pastor Tim's vision was to see the Fleming Campus have an Office of Operations and to launch one campus per year for the next five years. One of the campuses, the Downtown Campus, would be in conjunction with the building of a Dream Center to serve the poor and homeless people in the community. The Center would provide a way for them to have their physical needs met, hear the gospel, and have their hopes renewed.

Since they had just worked through the *No Limits* campaign six months prior, there was a potential for serious pushback. Would the church members be fundraising fatigued with the challenge of giving to the expansion? With this in mind, Pastor Tim shared the story of Philip and the Eunuch from the book of Acts, hoping to inspire the kind of attitude the congregation would need to fuel this vision of growth. The second campaign was called *Run for One.*

Pastor Tim assured the congregation that Philip must have been fatigued from his work in the gospel when God swept him away to share the gospel to the Ethiopian official. However, when God told Philip to go, Philip ran after the chariot in obedience. In the same way, Pastor Tim encouraged his church members that they needed to be willing to run after just one person in their area of Florida with the gospel by growing the church. By throwing off complacency and being ready to ask whether there was more they could give, they would be able to see God reaching the lost and hopeless.

This campaign was launched on a Sunday morning, preceded by commitments from key donors who pledged generous amounts. Those who weren't giving regularly were encouraged to give at least $100 a month, and those who were already regular givers were challenged to consider whether they could give twice that much. The members were encouraged to give in this way for 90 days and to record what God had been doing in their lives over that time.

PASSION FROM AN ETERNAL PERSPECTIVE

The church members gave $227,266 in its "starting line" offering that Sunday morning. In their two-year "expanded giving" campaign they received commitments for $1,742,000, far ahead of their goal.

The church members are well on their way toward keeping their donation commitments. Elevate Life has continued to grow throughout the struggles of fundraising campaigns. In 2015, Elevate Life Church baptized 319 people. Outreach Magazine noted the church as one of the 100 fastest growing churches in America. At the beginning of 2016, they averaged around 2,000 in attendance and were continuing with plans to open St. John's Campus in the fall of 2016 and the Downtown Campus in 2017.Their two back-to-back campaigns, while potentially grueling, were measurably successful. It will be instructive to see how they continue in the next few years.

Pastor Mark attributes their success to the tight-knit relationship between the staff members at Elevate Life and to Pastor Tim's ability to inspire people. It seems counter-intuitive, but people want to be challenged to be a part of something that is significant and bigger than themselves. Emphasizing the eternal perspective of sharing the gospel of Christ, reminding the church members of their own blessings through joining with Elevate Life, and communicating the optimism of what they could do together were all integral to the message. Passion is contagious.

The success of the two fundraising campaigns and subsequent growth of Elevate Life Church were rooted in leaders reminding church members of how they had been blessed by God since joining Elevate Life and communicating the optimism of what they could do together for others. Their hearts were moved, and they gave back vertically from what they had already been given.

While people can be tough to convince when there is a difficult task ahead, the irony is that people aren't inspired by small dreams that take little faith. Not to diminish the diligent work of Pastor Tim and the Elevate Life leadership team, but we should be careful to remember and praise the providence of God in blessing the growth of the Elevate Life Church.

QUESTIONS TO CONSIDER

- Can church leaders inspire and equip churches to do the impossible? That's what unreasonable churches do.

- What smoldering coals of potential can you fan into flame?

- What lies are you—or members of your church—possibly believing about capital campaigns?

- What scriptural basis can be used to combat these lies?

TAKEAWAY POINTS TO ACT ON:

1. *Don't be afraid of taking on challenges.* Leaders in a crisis rise to the occasion and challenge others to do the same even if it means taking the hard road. It is unreasonable and not recommended to do two major giving campaigns within a year. However, sometimes God's people need to do what seems unreasonable and not recommended.

2. *Don't underestimate the power of individuals.* If you see something that needs to be done (you have a "vision" of how the gospel can be served by your church), don't undervalue the ability of your church members to be inspired

to contribute to an eternally worthwhile project, even if they have already been giving themselves.

3. *Don't imply that giving is a "golden ticket" to God's favor.* Be careful not to make generosity a means of righteousness in your messages to your congregation. It is one thing to spur them on to good works; it is another to urge them to give in order to receive God's blessings.

4. *Excellent communication facilitates excellent things.* Elevate Life Church was very effective in its communication. They used personal meetings and online social media effectively. They kept members apprised of what was happening in their campaigns and continually invited new people by using online ads.

5. *Help the church see the "why" and "how."* When you describe what you want the church to accomplish with a capital campaign, be sure you are communicating why and how as well. You should be able to motivate people with true Biblical purpose that what you are doing is the church's work of evangelism and discipleship.

6. *Integrity and accountability are everything.* People can get very nervous when churches ask them to donate money. Make sure that everyone involved is doing this for the right

reasons. Allow questions to be asked, and answer them honestly. Be radically transparent and provide regular reports on how you are investing people's gifts. Let those potential donors know that the money they give will be handled with faithfulness. Develop a regular system of thanking people.

Chapter 2:

UNREASONABLE SELFLESSNESS

MOST PEOPLE ARE familiar with Isaac Newton's famous encounter with a falling apple—the image that we associate with Newton's law of gravity presented first in the 1600s. The laws of gravity revolutionized astronomical studies. But there is another little-known man instrumental in this discovery, Edmund Halley. Without Halley, no one would have ever heard about (or benefitted from) Newton.

Halley challenged Newton. He propelled Newton to think through his original philosophies, correcting Newton's mathematical mistakes and preparing geometric figures to support what he discovered. It was Halley who convinced Newton to put pen to paper and write his infamous Mathematical Principles of Natural Philosophy.

Mr. Halley acted as editor, supervised the entire process of publication and even financed the printing (though Newton was the wealthier of the two!). Historians have referred to Halley as "one of the most selfless examples in the annals of science." Newton benefitted from the rewards and prominence, but Halley received no accolades. Though Halley used this principle to predict the orbit and return of a comet that would later bear his name (Halley's Comet), Halley didn't receive one lick of acclaim until after he died. And unfortunately, Halley's Comet only returns every seventy-six years—almost unnoticed in the science world. But Halley, who remained a dedicated scientist for the remainder of his life, didn't care who received the credit; he was more concerned that the cause was advancing.

According to C.S. Kirkendall Jr., many biblical characters acted like Halley. First is John the Baptist, who said of Jesus, "He must become greater; I must become less." This truly is unreasonable selflessness. Barnabus too was content to introduce others to greatness. He was an early disciple in the New Testament church, a Levite from Cyprus (who was known as "Son of Encouragement" by Luke). Barnabas sold crops from his fields, giving the money to the Jerusalem apostles. Such selflessness advances the kingdom! Both John and Barnabas exhibited the kind of selflessness that is necessary for God's kingdom to expand here on earth.

THE ULTIMATE SELFLESS GIFT

The church of Jesus Christ was birthed out of such a timeless and selfless gift. The eternal God Almighty humbled Himself to become the human child of a lowly Jewish woman. The God-Man did this to accomplish the unreasonable—

exchanging the glories of heaven for misery and

suffering on behalf of people who hated Him. Jesus didn't just lay down His life for His friends, but for His enemies.

To the church, what Christ did for the world was simply unbelievable. The church proclaims that this unbelievable message transforms the hardest, most selfish heart into the most humble of givers.

Selflessness is one of the most important traits Christians can possess—so significant that Jesus lists it as the second most important of all of God's commandments! After Jesus had told His disciples the greatest commandment of all is to "Love the Lord your God with all your heart and with all your soul and with all your strength and with all your mind," His very next words were, "Love your neighbor as yourself" (Mark 12:31 NIV). In His Sermon on the Mount, Jesus took examples like helping a friend or caring for a child and extended that selfless attitude beyond what was normal. He called people to love their enemies and pray for those who persecute and hate them!

As followers of Jesus, in His image and as lights to a dark world, and because Christians are "of the same mind" as Christ, this is the attitude we too should have toward others. But do we walk the talk? Do churches actually live out this kind of selflessness in the real world of money and property? It might be rare, but the *unreasonable* church, like Christ himself, gives it all away. Are you leading like Jesus—not to be served but to *serve*?

FROM CHILDREN'S MINISTRY
TO NEW SOLUTIONS

Mountainside Gospel Chapel was established almost 200 years ago, in 1821, primarily to minister to children as Locust Grove Sunday School. In those early years, Gospel Chapel moved twice and ended up in the New Jersey borough of Mountainside. At its peak, the church grew to a membership of around 200 families as a vibrant church, which taught God's Word and ministered in the community. Their numbers stayed fairly consistent for about 150 years. After that, things began to change for the church.

In the 1970s the Mountainside Gospel Chapel started experiencing a slow but steady decline. The church continued to serve faithfully, but memberships continued to dwindle over the next 40 years. Eventually, they found themselves left with only 29 members. Like many other small, older churches in North America, they had difficult decisions to make.

With only 29 members, they couldn't continue to pay for the upkeep and running of the church facilities. So, under the leadership of their pastor, Dr. Gregg Hagg, they carefully considered their options. In many cases, churches in this situation have sold the property to another church, closed the doors, or declared bankruptcy. Gospel Chapel decided to consider a merger first.

Dr. Hagg had been contacting churches in their area over the past few years, asking whether they knew of any successful church mergers. In each case, the answer was always a discouraging, "No." All of the examples he heard involved two failing churches that merged, neither bringing vitality nor young people to the other and they together continued the slow spiral of death. The data about church mergers was not promising, but it did offer clues to the reasons the mergers failed. As Mountainside Gospel Chapel neared a time of urgency in their need to make a decision, they heard that Liquid Church was seeking a new place from which to launch.

One of the church elder's daughter had been part of the gospel-centered multi-site Liquid Church from its beginning. She told her dad that Liquid was looking for a place to meet in the Mountainside area of New Jersey, and they were facing challenges finding a suitable facility. On hearing that Liquid Church was searching for a place, the elders and Dr. Hagg discussed the possibility of working out a merger with the other leaders of Mountainside Gospel Chapel.

Dr. Hagg knew Liquid Church was one of the most vibrant congregations in the area. Their desire was to saturate the state of New Jersey with the gospel message. Launched by Tim Lucas and his team in 2007 with 300 members in Morristown, New Jersey, Liquid Church took its name from the concept of Christ being the water of life and that people coming to church should be refreshed. It was a congregation of mostly young people and young families, many of whom were new Christians, or had come back to Christ after walking away from the church of their youth. Liquid had grown to over 2,000 members at multiple sites when Dr. Hagg contacted them.

The day before he was approached by Mountainside Gospel Chapel, Pastor Lucas and his staff met with Warren Bird, author of *Better Together: Making Church Mergers Work.* Warren handed Pastor Lucas a copy of his book and asked the pastor to consider whether a merger could be within God's future for Liquid. Setting aside the book, Pastor Lucas had no real sense of investigating a merger model for Liquid's next launch.

The phone call from Mountainside Gospel Chapel and their offer to make their site the newest campus for Liquid Church astounded Pastor Tim. It seemed to him that this might be God at work, and he ought to at least pursue it. Tim set a meeting with Mountainside Gospel Chapel to find out more. To his amazement, he discovered that they wanted to sign over their church's facilities to Liquid Church because they were excited about what the young church was doing, and they wanted to join them in their work. The property that Gospel Chapel was offering to Liquid Church was worth $4,000,000. It was indeed a very generous offer, and the offer came with a desire to serve, not sit on the sidelines.

Liquid Church had not been considering purchasing any property in the area. They had been considering leasing because of the lesser financial burden. By offering to sign over the facilities to Liquid Church, Mountainside Gospel Chapel enabled the young church to consider the possibility of owning their church building in that community. The leadership of both churches met together and received wise counsel regarding the merging of the two churches. When

Mountainside Gospel Chapel took a vote on the matter, the vote was 29 for and none against—the proof of complete unity and unreasonable selflessness.

REBIRTH AND RENEWAL

Humbled by the generosity of Mountainside Gospel's offer, Liquid Church accepted the gift and began a 13-month process of renovating and refurbishing the old building for the launching of their Mountainside site the following year.

As they updated, repaired, and modernized some parts of the church, they decided to keep some elements that represented the history and ministry of the church's past. The beautiful stained glass windows would have a place in the refurbished building as a way to respect the members who had gone before them. At the same time, they replaced outdated equipment and added new technologies to facilitate modern media. They also made sure to have plenty of meeting spaces, rooms for teaching children, and even special facilities where children with autism could be in a one-on-one, calm environment with a caring adult while their parents attended services.

The members from Mountainside Gospel Chapel worked alongside Liquid Church in the updates of the church. In their minds, they were not merely handing over the church but were also becoming one with Liquid Church's ministry. On the day the new church was launched in the fall of 2013, the members of Mountainside Gospel Chapel were amazed and touched as over 1,000 people in four services poured into the refurbished facility. "This is what we wanted from this," said the original members of the church site. "This is what we wanted," as the tears poured down their faces.

Both members of Mountainside Gospel and members of Liquid Church were blessed by the love they saw poured out between their churches. In just 13 months, Mountainside Gospel Chapel's facilities went up from 29 church members to 1,300 on the first Easter Sunday, and they have continued to grow. By being willing to risk a merger, rather than close the doors and sell out, Mountainside Gospel Chapel enabled Liquid Church to have a large facility in the town from which to reach that community. By being willing to be involved in the transition, launch, and life of the church, Gospel Chapel members experienced its rebirth first hand and rejoiced in it.

UNITY OF SPIRIT

The selflessness displayed between these churches reminds us of what Biblical unity looks and acts like. Let's consider what the apostle Paul says:

> Therefore if there is any encouragement in Christ, if there is any consolation of love, if there is any fellowship of the Spirit, if any affection and compassion, make my joy complete by being of the same mind, maintaining

the same love, united in spirit, intent on one purpose. Do nothing from selfishness or empty conceit, but with humility of mind regard one another as more important than yourselves; do not merely look out for your own personal interests, but also for the interests of others. Have this attitude in yourselves which was also in Christ Jesus, who, although He Existed in the form of God, did not regard equality with God a thing to be grasped, but emptied Himself, taking the form of a bond-servant, and being made in the likeness of men. Being found in appearance as a man, He humbled Himself by becoming obedient to the point of death, even death on a cross.

– PHILIPPIANS 2:1–8 NASB

The members of Mountainside Gospel and Liquid Church displayed humility toward one another and a spirit of selflessness in their desire to further the gospel and lift each other up. Even in choosing a church to merge with, Dr. Hagg and the members of Mountainside Gospel Chapel considered Liquid Church because of its fervor for the gospel of Christ. On both sides, they took on the attitude of Christ as He came to the world to gave His life for the world. The commitment to the gospel, trust in God's leading, and an attitude of respect and mutual submission made possible the unity of spirit that made this merger so beautifully successful.

QUESTIONS TO CONSIDER

- Are you leading your church toward this kind of unreasonable selflessness?

- What would the world think if they saw churches with the mindset and actions of Christ?

- How does the attitude of your church toward other churches in the area compare to the posture between Mountainside Gospel Chapel and Liquid Church?

TAKEAWAY POINTS TO ACT ON:

1. *Churches have a "lifespan."* People may not want to realize it, but just as churches are born, they can reach a time when they die. This is within the sovereign providence of God. It can be easy to think of multiple reasons for a church's decline, but times and neighborhoods and cultures change. What if God is using the death of one to give life to another? That sounds familiar.

2. *Church success is about faithfulness to the gospel of Christ not butts in chairs.* Perhaps the most profound lesson of this story is that Dr. Hagg's little church was so heavenly minded that they were the greatest example of earthly good. The world may choose to

cash out and divide the profits, but imitators of Christ seek the continuation of the timeless gospel message. Only by God's grace can we possess this kind of Christ-like humility.

3. *Mergers should be looked at more carefully.* The economics of the modern world will mean that more and more churches will be in Mountainside Gospel's position. What if this rebirth could be a model and example for others to follow?

4. *Humility is the most important virtue of a Christian leader.* The humility of both sides of this merger is the most stunning aspect of this story. In a Christian culture where pastors are held up in the cult of personality, these men humbled themselves enough to listen to their churches, wise advisors, each other, and mostly, to the leadership of the Lord.

5. *There is no generation gap among Christians.* A growing "elephant in the room" is the supposed disconnect between older and newer church tools and methodologies. Many older churches do not want to be dragged into the technologies of the 21st century, and many newer churches have an arrogance attached to their youth. This story reveals that the disconnect is based on pride and it is false.

6. *Selfless is the most unreasonable thing a church could be.* Perhaps if churches were more unreasonable in this way, we could win the world to Christ!

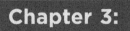

UNREASONABLE CONNECTIONS

PAUL LAWRENCE WORKS on the assembly line at the Hyundai plant in Montgomery, Alabama. During one of his breaks, he was watching a YouTube video on his phone about basic tennis lessons. Another worker, Jamal Henry, overheard the video and sat down across from Paul. "Sounds like you're a tennis player," Jamal said with a smile. Paul looked up from his phone with a grunt. "Well, I don't know that I would say that. But tennis is my thing. I'm trying to be more active, you know." The two men introduced themselves and Jamal extended an invitation.

"Listen, I am a tennis player as well" Jamal started. "I play with a group every Tuesday evening at the Hampstead courts. We're not pros or anything, but we have a lot of fun, and we would love to have you come. What do you think?" Paul accepted that invitation to the Drop Shot Tennis Group. And with that simple invitation, Paul embarked on a new journey in life. Eventually, Jamal invited Paul to join him one Sunday at church.

What began in the factory break room would be completed in the last place Paul ever expected to go—an *unreasonable* church, a massive church that connects people together through small groups of all shapes and interests.

JESUS' LEADERSHIP TEAM

Though it may seem like a pretty hands-off way to train new leaders, this way of learning within the context of playing and working together is not new. In fact, the true "creator" of this leadership method is none other than Jesus.

In fact, the original twelve disciples Jesus chose lacked background, education, and vocational aptitude for the huge enterprise they would soon undertake! Seminary, college professor, and writer Pastor Gene Getz, in a humorous email poking fun at the criteria people classically use to select leaders, writes this "assessment" of the men Jesus chose—as if they were applying for management positions:

> Simon Peter is emotionally unstable and given to fits of temper. Andrew has no qualities of leadership. The two brothers, James and John, sons of Zebedee, place personal interests above company loyalty. Thomas demonstrates a questioning attitude that would tend to undermine morale. We feel it our duty to tell you that Matthew has been blacklisted by the Greater Jerusalem Better Business Bureau. James, the son of Alphaeus, and particularly Simon the Zealot have radical leanings, and they both registered a high score

on the manic-depressive scale. Thaddaeus is definitely sensitive, but he wants to make everyone happy.

One of the candidates, however, shows great potential. He is a man of ability and resourcefulness, meets people well, has a keen business mind, and has contacts in high places. He is highly motivated, ambitious, and responsible. We recommend Judas Iscariot as your controller and right-hand man. All of the other profiles are self-explanatory. We wish you every success in your new venture.[2]

Humorous—and borderline true! Jesus devoted himself to this small motley group of men, young and uneducated, and daily spent time with them. Then, after His death and resurrection, He left them with a commission to "go and make disciples of all nations." These "group leaders," had received a mere three years of training before they began leading their own "groups," and most of it occurred over meals and while traveling. But these very first small groups would be catalysts that would change the world, with the Holy Spirit as their "coach" along the way.

The very day after Jesus was baptized, John the Baptizer saw Jesus and said to His disciples, "Look, the Lamb of God!" (John 1:35 NIV). When two of John's disciples heard John say this, they followed Jesus, who invited them to "come ... and you will see" (John 1:39).

---

2 Gene A. Getz, *The Apostles* (Nashville: Broadman & Holman, 1998), pp. 3-4.

Little did they know, but those two men had found their Messiah.

This is what Jamal did with Paul Lawrence; he invited him to "come and see."

When Paul first attended the "Drop Shots Tennis Group", he connected with people who place the Lord first in their lives—not tennis—and his life changed forever.

CONNECTING THE MULTITUDES

Chris Hodges planted Church of the Highlands in Birmingham, Alabama, in 2001. Pastor Chris not only planted a church, but with the help and inspiration of several others, a new model of church planting was born as well. These men included Greg Surratt at Seacoast Church, Rick Bezet (who launched a church in Arkansas on the same day as Pastor Chris), and Billy Hornsby, Pastor Chris' father-in-law.

In the process of planting Church of the Highlands, they created ARC (the Association of Related Churches) to support the continued launching of churches and the spread of the gospel. They believed this new process would be more effective than the older models. Their strategies worked in the planting of the Birmingham church, so they continued to expand the ministry of ARC. The organization has helped to plant over 600 churches in the last 15 years. The stunning growth of Church of the Highlands has been an ongoing testimony to the success of ARC. 38,000 people attend Church of the Highlands weekly services online and at 14 campuses.

The need for people to feel connected to others runs deep and universal. One study revealed that even being ignored by a group that a person wants nothing to do with has the possibility of making them feel left out! How much more, then, will someone feel left out when not connected to the people they worship with at church?

How does this church connect with and keep track of 38,000 individuals? That's the size of a small city. Indeed, there are only 15 cities in Alabama with a population larger than Church of the Highlands! With such a large crowd, even spread out over 14 locations, organizing small groups is essential to connect the people of Highlands together. To have so many small groups, and training and organizing group leaders and volunteers requires an army of logistical leaders. Even in small churches, it can be a challenge to recruit and train small group leaders. In larger churches, multiple staff positions are often needed to organize church members into small groups and train the group leaders.

Most churches only have pre-set kinds of groups which come from the leadership. But when you're dealing with tens of thousands, how do you find enough niches to fit each individual? Breaking the large church into effective small groups is a constant challenge.

CHURCH OUTSIDE THE BOX

Having been instrumental in breaking the mold of church planting, Pastor Chris and Church of the

Highlands proceeded to break the mold of small group ministry. They developed the concept of *Free Market Small Groups* to deal with the challenges inherent in small group formation, emphasizing trust in God's working, mentorship, and empowering their members. In the *Free Market* system of small groups, the members who host small groups choose the topic of study, when and where to meet, and what their group does. The Church does not dictate what the small groups will be and doesn't create a complicated structure and meeting agenda for these groups.

The *Free Market* idea works because the group members are more passionate about their group. The group leaders are interested and experienced in the focus of the group, and are enthusiastic about inviting others to join their group. The group members and leaders may naturally have more contacts in the areas of their interest and have more success in asking new people to come. Additionally, when members are interested and engaged in the group, they are less likely to become burned out.

This *Free Market* structure for small groups also allows for the ebb and flow of the seasons, life schedules, and individual interests. The small groups at Highlands take breaks that coincide with school calendars, for instance. The sessions run much like school semesters, taking December off, and then restarting again in January. Rather than running small groups the entire summer, the session is shorter, just about a month long.

Highlands has developed an extensive online

directory of small groups, listed under general categories. Church members looking for a group to join can choose the category, location, and see options for which group they may choose. Currently, the website lists 31 different categories with multiple groups offered in each category. Information about the group can be seen online, and potential group members can email the leader through the online directory. The directory can be viewed at https://groups.highlandsapp.com/

Perhaps the best measurement of the *Free Market* small group model is the high rate of small group attendance. Church of the Highlands respects the gifts the members bring to the church, and they recognize the community that comes from meeting and working with like-minded people. They also trust in the work of the Holy Spirit to continue to work in their member's lives within the context of the church's weekly Biblical instruction. (One category of small groups is a discussion of the sermon of the previous weekend.) By providing a coach, the leaders aren't left hanging, while also not overwhelming the leaders with hours of pre-training. The effect, in turn, is small group leaders who feel appreciated, empowered, enthusiastic and equipped.

UNREASONABLE LEADERSHIP TRAINING

The way that Church of the Highlands addresses the training of small group leaders may seem radically hands-off compared to many churches. Highlands believes that more training classes and lessons don't always work out toward better-trained leaders. The church asks the small group leaders to attend a 4-step Growth Track, which is four 1-hour classes intended to assimilate potential leaders into the church, discover their purpose, and during the last week, be trained as a Small Group Leader. There are two expectations of every leader:

1. Spiritually identify every person in your group (where are they in their relationship with God, anywhere from a non-Christian to a mature Christian).

2. During the small group session (or semester), help that person move just one step forward in their relationship with Christ. There's no pressure to bring someone vast distances, just one step, if possible.

Once they have been through the Growth Track, each leader is assigned a coach to turn to for guidance. Then, the group leaders are encouraged to learn as they begin leading their groups. It's within the context of actual small group leadership that most of the leadership training happens. If the group host has concerns or needs advice, the coach is available for wisdom and encouragement. In addition, online resources are available for continual self-paced training.

Church of the Highlands' leadership believes that hands-on learning is more effective than having an intense study of information without the ability to apply it immediately. Having an ongoing coach is crucial to the Free Market small groups system. The coach is available when things are going well, but more importantly, the mentor is there to help in times of crisis or struggle. Those moments tend to be the most valuable opportunities for the growth of the leader. Going up the ladder of accountability, the coach, in turn, can approach the church leadership for counsel and wisdom.

In most cases the group leader will not choose to teach, but if they want to, the church has resources available. The nature of effective small groups, however, is that more is "caught" than "taught." Learning happens very effectively in the context of playing and working together.

Apostle Paul's method of leadership was not unlike the Free Market method. Paul prepared and trained workers to continue the groups he had started, city to city. He acted as a "coach." To Titus, he sent instruction, and to Timothy, encouragement. He delegated responsibility to the leaders of those groups. Then, he watched, listened, intervened when necessary, and let them fly!

QUESTIONS TO CONSIDER

- How are you connecting people like Paul to your church?

- How are you connecting lives like Jamal and Paul to each other?

- How does your church identify and train leaders? Is this current method effective?

TAKEAWAY POINTS TO ACT ON:

1. *Check out the Free Market model.* One of the primary goals at Church of the Highlands for their small groups model is that it would be scalable; that the new campus launches with smaller numbers would be able to use this model, and the small groups would be able to continue no matter how large the church grew. For this reason, they feel that their small groups plan can be helpful to churches of any size. They even provide material online to assist churches in making use of their Free Market small groups model. Here's the link to the online resource: www.growleader.com

2. *Large crowd energy might bring them in, but small group connection will keep them there.* Highlands understands that every one of the 38,000 people is an individual with different

interests and life situations. For small groups, one size does not fit all.

3. *Effective and ongoing leader training is crucial to effective small groups.* A small group leader at Highlands knows the how and why of training. The combination of the Growth Track, an available and caring coach, and on-the-job training makes the task of group leadership attainable.

4. *Valuing and trusting leaders are the keys to effective volunteer management.* Highlands would not be able to manage these many small groups. Trusting leaders to do the work God has called them to do in their groups will strengthen the groups more and more.

5. *If it's not scalable, it's probably not doable.* The beauty of this system is that next year, there might be 20 more small group leaders available with 20 different interests. As long as the church is discipling and growing more leaders, there will always be new small groups as the church grows.

6. *Even though it's unreasonable, it might be the most effective.* In their small group ministry, Highlands values the connections between people most of all. They have one purpose for small groups, and that is to bring people together. Maybe the groups are

not Bible study focused or lesson based, but
the relationships established in the small
groups become the glue that holds the 38,000
together.

Chapter 4

UNREASONABLE SERVICE

A MAN NAMED CARL met with some city leaders who had been invited to meet together to begin planning for city transformation. It was a very exciting group; but one of the leaders of a major organization couldn't meet because of a personal problem in his family. Several people from that organization, however, did attend. As they began planning and committing resources and strategies, the organization's people were right there committing their organization and its resources without ever having to run to a phone and call their leader.

Later, as Carl was traveling back to his hotel on a city bus with one member of that large organization, he commented about what a beautiful example of servant leadership he had witnessed, and how it impressed him. "I don't often see it in Christian organizations," Carl marveled. "Yes," the staffer said. "What you saw is the way we work. If a visitor comes in and asks for the top man, our boss will probably point to one of the others and keep working.

A young church staffer, just out of college, receives her first assignment at her new job: go talk to the city park board and see what the church can do to fill the city's volunteer needs. Her second assignment: go talk to the mayor's office and find out what the church can do to help serve the city.

What kind of church hires a staffer to do this kind of work? What kind of church allows staffers to make major decisions, without the approval of the man at the top?

An *unreasonable* church with an unreasonable passion to serve people in the name of Christ.

MINISTRY—A GROUP EFFORT

At one point in Jesus' ministry, just after He learned that His cousin John had been beheaded, the Bible says Jesus "withdrew to a boat privately to a solitary place" (Matt. 14:13 NIV). However, the crowds followed him. Jesus, gripped with compassion, healed their sick.

But the crowds continued to come, and Jesus' disciples were growing discouraged. Matthew recounts the story:

> As evening approached, the disciples came to him and said, "This is a remote place, and it's already getting late. Send the crowds away, so they can go to the villages and buy themselves some food." Jesus replied, "They do not need to go away. You give them something to eat."
>
> "We have here only five loaves of bread and two fish," they answered.
>
> "Bring them here to me," he said. And he directed the people to sit down on the grass. Taking the five loaves and the two fish and looking up to heaven, he gave thanks and

broke the loaves. Then he gave them to the disciples, and the disciples gave them to the people. They all ate and were satisfied, and the disciples picked up twelve basketfuls of broken pieces that were left over. The number of those who ate was about five thousand men, besides women and children.

– MATTHEW 14:15-21 (NIV)

Jesus could have caused a banquet to appear at the snap of His fingers, but instead He tells His disciples, "*You* give them something to eat" (Matt. 14:16b, emphasis added). Jesus involves them. He engages them in the miracle and in doing so the experience likely left them speechless—and forever changed.

A CHURCH BORN TO SERVE

Twenty years ago, Pastor Mike Linch and Pastor Ike Reighard planted the NorthStar Church in Kennesaw, Georgia. The church began as a church for people who didn't go to church. At that time, there was only one other church startup in their area, and NorthStar was considered a pioneer in church planting. From the beginning, Pastor Mike and the leadership team had a desire to reach out to their community through service. They wanted to be seen as a blessing to the people of their city, whether those they served were members of the church or not.

Pastor Mike has created a culture of service built into the foundation of the church. A vast majority of the members have not grown up in church or didn't have any kind of solid church history. Getting involved with "church stuff" is new to them, especially volunteering to serve.

A constant struggle for the active church is the attempt to fit their programs in between various community activities that members are involved in. The pace of modern life is busy, and churches frequently add to that busyness. From school and sports activities for families to community and business events, it can be tricky to find an opening in the calendar for weeknight meetings or any other kind of activities. People can only do so much.

Most churches are program driven. They schedule their buildings full of Bible studies and youth events, which may or may not have much turnout based on the members' pace of life. This can be a frustrating conundrum for churches, causing bitterness and burnout for the church leadership, pastors, and volunteers. Programs for large churches require tons of volunteers. As a congregation full of faith newbies, finding volunteers for all those programs was a daunting task.

NorthStar wanted a better way than the grind of weekly programs staffed by too-busy over-committed and under-confident servants.

UNREASONABLE SERVANTS

Instead of creating a calendar full of church-centered events that compete with the community's schedule,

NorthStar actively encourages church members to spend their time volunteering in community-centered activities. The church promotes community volunteerism to church members. Almost every night of the month, there are various opportunities to serve listed on the NorthStar website.

One of the ministries is taking a warm cup of coffee to chemo patients. Another ministry is just playing Bingo with elderly people at an assisted living facility. They help out and encourage the schools and take low-income kids on field trips. Volunteers can serve the local food pantries and homeless shelters. There are an incredible number of ways to serve the community through the church. NorthStar works with individuals, organizations, schools, and even the local government community programs. While many churches sponsor their own youth sports leagues, NorthStar supports the city parks and recreation programs with volunteers. The church will adopt a team and provide volunteers throughout the sports season.

The process of discovering needs begins with each New Year. They approach the community leaders working in social services, schools, sports leagues, and city programs, and ask, "What can we do to help you assist the community? We have volunteers ready to serve."

But NorthStar's service commitment is more than just a token attempt to show a slight community interest. They put their money where their mouth is. They pay people to do nothing but coordinate volunteers doing work outside the church. The congregation demonstrates their commitment to community service by keeping two full-time staff members who specialize in community outreach. The staff members determine the needs and make the opportunities known to the church.

The culture of service is so deeply embedded into the life of NorthStar that the facility itself gives priority scheduling to outside community groups. Since the church is not program driven, freeing up their members' time has also freed up the church building schedule. Instead of having the building sit empty most days of the year, the church allows community groups and organizations to hold events and meetings for free. Church staff and members host the events as if the meeting space was rented and staff hired to serve as hosts.

In 2013, 150 community activities were held at NorthStar's facility. Each of those events had 250 people or more in attendance. This church has become known for having open doors in the community.

AN INDISPENSABLE CHURCH

The local church used to be the center of everything that happened in a community. As the culture has drastically changed, the church is seen more and more as just irrelevant to life. NorthStar's model has demonstrated that churches can free their members to move out of the church and into their community, and at the same time, allow the community to come into the church. This church has encouraged an effective way for Christians to mingle with others and share the gospel as they work and play and volunteer together.

NorthStar wanted to be seen as the church that is *indispensable* in the community, not the church that is *invisible*. That is what they aimed at, and that is what they have achieved with their community-centered mindset. Each year, thousands of people enter NorthStar's facility and have an excellent experience with the church. The church firmly believes that some of those individuals who are not Christians will feel more at home with the thought of coming to a Sunday service. Whether they come back on Sunday or not, one thing will be clear to them; the church is open and generous with its property and time.

But it's not just the church *building* that is indispensable to the community. The church *people* are indispensable as servants and volunteers. NorthStar members enjoy having the freedom and ministry of serving the community in the context of the church facilities or in the larger community. They recognize that the work they do outside of the walls of the church is also the work of the church: being the hands and feet of Christ to a world that needs His love. Whether it's serving at a homeless shelter, helping a child with special needs at a ball game, cooking breakfast for high-school students, or hosting a meeting space for teachers to plan the next school year, volunteers see the tangible value of giving their time. As a volunteer-oriented church, serving *outside* the church often leads members to be willing to serve *inside* the church on Sunday morning in various ways.

Something happens when God's people become involved in unreasonable service for God. They see God. They experience God. They experience His presence as He ministers to others, through them. And there is no "experience requirement" for even the newest believer in Jesus! They only need to be available to serve. A person is never more like Christ than when they are serving others: "For even the Son of Man came not to be served but to serve, and to give his life as a ransom for many" (Mark 10:45).

This is the heartbeat of Christ, and the heartbeat of an unreasonable church.

QUESTIONS TO CONSIDER

- Does your church exist to serve or to be served?

- Are your facilities and schedule prioritized so that the community gets first dibs?

- What would your church need to stop doing to make room for this sort of community service?

TAKEAWAY POINTS TO ACT ON:

1. *Consider the volunteer efforts at your church.* Too often, churches can fall into the trap of guilt-tripping people into volunteering. Do your efforts to recruit and support volunteers create thoughts of love and joy or painful duty? Christians should be encouraged to serve from the motivation of love and pleasing their heavenly Father. If the motivation is guilt, self-justification, or even for church marketing, it will be evident to those being served.

2. *Is it necessarily true that 20 percent of the people do 80 percent of the work?* Perhaps the reason churches struggle so much with recruiting volunteers is because 80 percent of the work seems vain and worthless. If the volunteering of time and energy went to a more

community-centered model, could volunteers see more value in their donated time?

3. *Start small.* Many churches may not have the means to hire full-time community outreach staff, but there are ways to begin. Meet with the school to see how the church can open its doors to planning meetings. Talk to another leader in the city and ask how the church can help them make things better in the community. The key is to have the spirit of a servant, not a competitor for time and space.

4. *Use the resources you have.* Most churches have some facilities that could be utilized by the community. Additionally, most churches have people who are hired to clean the church. Train that person to be a host and a servant to community groups meeting in the church. Having a host on hand makes it clear that the church is open-handed with its property and wants to serve in any way that it can.

5. *Go to the people you know need the most support.* Go to the mayor or parks and recreation department and offer to help meet needs. Ask them, "What are your needs and how can we help?" Asking the question may open up opportunities you wouldn't have thought of before. Taking the time to ask the school

principal, the police officers, the food pantry, the mayor, or your neighbors how you can serve them is a good step toward becoming indispensable to the community.

6. *Consider all resources as tools, and people as precious.* Too often, churches are infamous for being consumers of human resources, not producers of human resources. At the same time, church property is often viewed as something to be protected at all costs. Is it possible that we have considered the resources as precious and the people as mere tools?

Chapter 5:

UNREASONABLE DISCIPLESHIP

JOURNALIST SHANE SNOW surveyed 3,000 people with this question: "Who would you trust more as your leader? J.K. Rowling or Queen Elizabeth?" The vast majority would rather follow the storyteller than the world leader. The famous proverb reveals why: "Those who tell the stories rule the world." This saying, attributed to Plato and to native Americans, describes why the most established storytelling juggernaut in the world, the Disney Corporation, continues to cause parents everywhere to hear *"Let It Go"* 35 times a day.

Stories are ultimately about people, with all the trials and victories that people blunder through. The storytellers themselves immerse their lives into their stories; just like the characters of their stories, they wander down life's unknown paths with doubts and fears. Who will reach these storytellers with the greatest Story of all? Only an *unreasonable* church!

THE POWER OF A STORY

There is something profound about storytelling. Recall that the vast majority of people would rather follow the storyteller than the world leader. In the second half of

Jesus' ministry, He suddenly began using parables to teach. The word "parable" is derived from two Greek words: *para*, meaning "beside" and *ballo*, meaning "to cast or throw." So then, a parable is literally something "cast alongside" something else— stories that were "cast alongside" a spiritual truth, to explain or illuminate it. A parable is usually a short, simple fictitious story that illustrates or communicates a spiritual truth, a moral lesson or a religious principle. They were teaching aids—earthly material stories with deeper spiritual meanings.

Sometimes people understood the stories Jesus taught, but other times people, like the Pharisees, didn't get them. They had a preconceived idea of who the Messiah should be, and passed off Jesus' parables as utter nonsense. But those who wanted to understand truth understood these parables. Sometimes for people in modern times, it's a bit tricky to interpret what Jesus' parables mean; other times, Jesus interprets the parable for us—like the Parable of the Sower and the Parable of the Wheat and the Weeds (Matt. 13). But the bottom line is this: parables moved something in the hearts of those who heard them, and caused them to rethink certain things about themselves.

The prophet Nathan in the Old Testament told one of the best-known parables in the Bible:

> The Lord sent Nathan to David. When he came to him, he said, "There were two men in a certain town, one rich and the other poor. The

rich man had a very large number of sheep and cattle, but the poor man had nothing except one little ewe lamb he had bought. He raised it, and it grew up with him and his children. It shared his food, drank from his cup and even slept in his arms. It was like a daughter to him.

"Now a traveler came to the rich man, but the rich man refrained from taking one of his own sheep or cattle to prepare a meal for the traveler who had come to him. Instead, he took the ewe lamb that belonged to the poor man and prepared it for the one who had come to him."

David burned with anger against the man and said to Nathan, "As surely as the Lord lives, the man who did this must die! He must pay for that lamb four times over because he did such a thing and had no pity."

Then Nathan said to David, "You are the man! This is what the Lord, the God of Israel, says: 'I anointed you king over Israel, and I delivered you from the hand of Saul. I gave your master's house to you, and your master's wives into your arms. I gave you all Israel and Judah. And if all this had been too little, I would have given you even more. Why did you despise the word of the Lord by doing what is evil in his eyes? You struck down Uriah the Hittite with the sword and took his wife to be your own. You killed him with the sword of the Ammonites. Now, therefore, the sword will never depart from your house because you despised me and took the wife of Uriah the Hittite to be your own.

– 2 Samuel 12:1–10 NIV

Nathan told a story to provoke David's confession of murdering Uriah and committing adultery with Uriah's wife, Bathsheba. Notice the story caused David to grow angry—that is until he realized his own sin.

Though it was a method of teaching in biblical times, stories are just as powerful and effective today. Stories make teachings easier to remember and apply, they endure far longer than sermons, and they encourage introspection and open up conversation—especially for people like those in Cast Member Church, whose story is told below.

People who don't come from a church background may begin to see what their purpose is best through this type of teaching. And in the process, many professional "storytellers" are coming to know the greatest *Storyteller* of all: Jesus.

A NEW TESTAMENT CHURCH

Cast Member Church—one church with three locations in Orlando, FL and Anaheim and Burbank, CA— is one of the most unique churches in North America. Steven Barr launched and pastors the church along with leaders at all three locations throughout the week. The focus and vision of Cast Member Church is to bring a Kingdom influence to every corner of The Walt Disney Company—the largest media company in the world. The Walt Disney Company employs over 100,000 people in all of its facilities, and the majority of the Cast Members do not attend church anywhere, nor are they Christians.

Cast Member Church gets its name from the title which the Disney Company gives to its employees. No matter what job they have at the parks and resorts, the workers are all called "cast members." Every employee has a role to play.

Pastor Steven had worked as a cast member for a season, and during that time, he thought, "It would be great if there was a church just for cast members." He had forgotten about this thought, but it came back to lead him to this one-of-a-kind ministry. Pastor Steven set out to reach cast members with the gospel of Jesus Christ, but he certainly had some obstacles ahead of him.

As he began efforts to establish the Cast Member Church, Pastor Steven spent several weeks meeting with church leaders in Orlando. He was trying to figure out what had worked and what had not worked from established churches trying to reach out to the employees at Disney. All he heard was horror stories of churches trying and failing. This group of people was so diverse and different. He quickly found out that a typical church model was not going to work.

As an entertainment park open 365 days a year, there was no way that the usual Sunday morning service was going to work. It would be like planting a church in Hollywood. Most of the cast members were young and church was not even on their radars. Pastor Steven had come up with plans on how he was going to create a church ministry for the cast. However, by the third week or so, after speaking to the local churches and receiving discouraging news, he had a moment of truth asking the Lord "What do you want me to do?"

In prayer, he decided to go back to the Bible to figure out what kind of ministry he should do to reach out the cast members at Disney World. He asked the question, "How did it work in the New Testament?" He studied the book of Acts and how the Lord grew the infant church. As he studied the Scriptures, he recalled what author Mike Breen said, "If you plant churches, you might get disciples, but if you make disciples, you always get the church."[3]

A MICRO-CHURCH OF DISCIPLES

So, to birth the unique Cast Member Church, Pastor Steven did it the old fashioned way. Trusting the truth of Scripture, his plan was to make disciples instead of planting a church for the cast members. He began this effort of unreasonable discipleship believing that as he made disciples, God would take care of the church. Pastor Steven began to gather a group of young cast members whom he taught, mentored, and discipled. These disciples, in turn, began to gather a group of people around themselves whom they also discipled. They named this network of groups, CommuniDs (D for Disney, or also for Discipleship).

To continue the growth of the Cast Member Church,

---

3 Building a Discipling Culture by Mike Breen

Pastor Steven began to enter the parks as a guest on an annual pass (Disney doesn't pay him, and he is not endorsed by Disney World). He connected with cast members at the Disney parks and hotels, as a paying guest, and engaged them in conversation. As cast members showed interest in the unique ministry, Pastor Steven invited them to the CommuniD groups.

The CommuniDs are "micro churches" of four or five cast members that meet at all kinds of times and places, mostly in hotels where the cast members can find a small quiet space. Some of them meet online. The CommuniD also functions as a family element, providing a secure relationship in which it's safe to share questions and doubts. Once a month, all the CommuniDs come together for a time of extended worship, prayer, and fellowship. Pastor Steven is constantly working to grow the network and expand the reach of the micro-church concept.

Every new group is introduced to *Life Beyond Imagination,* which Pastor Steven developed. *Life Beyond Imagination* is a process which provides a way to share about Jesus without having the conversation shut down before the gospel even comes up. Pastor Steven discovered early on that if he told cast members that he was a pastor, or talked about Jesus, then the conversation quickly ended. But alternatively, he found that cast members were very interested in talking about their purpose, and *Life Beyond Imagination* uses that route to introduce the gospel.

The series of conversations use "Disney speak" to talk

about finding their purpose in ways that the cast members relate to, using words such as "dream," "quest," and "story" to help them understand the significance of God's Word and His gospel in their lives. Cast members at Disney World often have these questions floating around in their heads: "Who am I?" "Why am I here?" "Where am I going?" "What does it even matter?" These issues open up the opportunity to share their purpose in Christ. In the process of introducing Christ, the lessons teach that each cast member has a purpose, but they have been separated from the One that gave them purpose. At their micro-church meetings, group leaders work with their CommuniD groups through this process of understanding their purpose in life and how the gospel of Jesus Christ relates to them.

DISCIPLING DISNEY

The Disney World cast members are listening to these lessons, and Pastor Steven is surprised by the amazing conversion rate. Indeed, the cast members who come to Christ already have the ability to communicate their message and speak to others because of the nature of the Disney cast member culture.

But Pastor Steven is doing more than converting people; he is *discipling* them. Disciples are followers of Jesus who have moved beyond a profession of faith, and into a lifelong pursuit of living like Jesus. Jesus commanded that all His followers go and "make disciples of all nations." It is not an extra activity for those Christians who have extra time or feel they are "called" to that area of service in the church, but rather what believers *are*. Jesus modeled it, teaching the masses but also investing in and training up disciples in both public and intimate moments. Paul taught about the importance of discipleship too saying, "The things you have heard me say in the presence of many witnesses entrust to reliable people who will also be qualified to teach others" (2 Tim. 2:2). When God's people invest in others, they grow too—the water of life flows out to the other person, but pours into the one doing the investing.

The members of Cast Member Church are dreamers and doers. These creative people, usually just out of college, want to make a difference in the world. Many of them are entertainers, merchandise sales people and food and beverage workers. The Cast Member Church works first of all to make disciples, and then those disciples learn to become disciple-makers themselves.

Pastor Steven looks to his cast members for ideas and inspiration rather than looking outside at other churches and their leaders. With such a different church, who better than the young disciple-makers to create new and innovative solutions to the challenges of ministry in the Disney theme parks?

Pastor Steven and the leadership at the Cast Members Church have a desire to launch a Cast Member Church at every Disney location. They have already begun in Anaheim, California, and they hope to spread this unique ministry to Disney properties around the world.

QUESTIONS TO CONSIDER

- Who will be creative and visionary enough to do the unreasonable?

- What unusual groups or "micro cultures" exist in your community, who need to know Jesus?

- Will you take up the gritty, determined mindset of the missionary and reach the unreachable?

TAKEAWAY POINTS TO ACT ON:

1. *What a crazy idea: look to the Scriptures about how to build the church.* When Pastor Steven went into the church plant at Disney World, he ran into some obstacles for his original vision for his launch. He realized his ideas wouldn't work. In prayer, Steven looked to God's Word and sought a solution for how a church could be planted among the cast members. He especially paid attention to accounts in Acts about the church and its establishment. His advice to church leaders is not necessarily to look at other churches for direction, although you may receive some insight from them. Use the Bible as your tool and main source of wisdom as you look at

the unique setting or group of people you are working with.

2. *Praying and reading the Bible actually works.* Pastor Steven offers an ancient but fresh perspective on church planting. The church is Jesus' church and His Word records that prayer and the work of the Holy Spirit are the keys for church planting.

3. *It's all about discipleship.* Many outwardly successful churches struggle with the concept of making disciples. This is the primary mission that Jesus established for the church, and yet it seems so foreign to many churches. As Pastor Steven quoted from author Mike Breen, "If you plant churches, you might get disciples, but if you make disciples, you always get the church."

4. *A micro-culture might need a micro-church.* Pastor Steven was drawn to these cast members because he loved them and understood them, but that doesn't mean that they would love and understand anything like a typical church. As someone who connected with the cast members, Pastor Steven was humble enough to rethink his methodology and listen to those whom he wanted to serve. It may be unreasonable, but it is fulfilling the Great Commission.

5. *Serving a micro culture is not simple or easy.* Although Pastor Steven is sometimes teased about doing "work" at such a fun place as the Disney parks, the establishment and continual growth of Cast Member Church was a matter of diligence and hard work. This missionary to the micro culture had to dig in and find the people God called him to serve. In the Internet age full of church planting advice, it is tempting to try to imitate. The hard work is to innovate to make discipleship happen in the microculture.

6. *Are there other micro-cultures that have been overlooked?* Pastor Steven's life experience gave him a unique ability to understand the cast member niche. What experiences do you have that could help serve other micro-cultures?

Chapter 6:

UNREASONABLE LOCATIONS

JEREMY RIDDLE CAME to Lubbock to study engineering at Texas Tech, but his car had broken down and he didn't have the money to fix it. He scraped by with a borrowed bike for months, and figured that it would just be cheaper to continue using a bike. Selling the car would help pay for his school bill, and where was he going to go, anyway? He didn't have time to go anywhere else, and he worked on campus with the maintenance crew.

A girl on the crew asked him to come check out her church. Not wanting to turn down an invite from a girl, and not wanting to bum a ride from her, he stumbled for the answer. "Oh, I don't know, I may not be able to get there."

"That's okay." She replied with a smile. "It's right here on campus. Tuesday night. See you there!"

To reach out to students on the college campus, the *unreasonable* church does what it takes to get the job done—including being creative in where to meet!

WORSHIP OVER "WHERE"

For many people, the word "church" brings images to mind of stained-glass windows, cold wooden pews and organs. The church is often considered to be a building but according to the Bible, this is not what a church *is.* The word "church" comes from a Greek word *ekklesia*, meaning, "a called-out assembly or congregation." It is an assembly (or group) of people called by God who gather together. Luke writes, "Every day they devoted themselves to meeting together *in the temple area* and to breaking bread *in their homes*" (Acts 2:46a, emphasis added). In the first few years after Jesus was resurrected, God's people met in homes, synagogues, and the temple to worship Him—there was no set place. In Acts 12:12, for example, God's people met in Mary's home:

> "When he [Peter] realized this, he went *to the house of Mary*, the mother of John who is called Mark, where there were many people gathered in prayer" (Acts 12:12, emphasis added).

Clearly, a worship gathering was taking place when Peter arrived! In Acts 16:40, after Paul and Silas were released from prison, they "went to Lydia's *house* where they saw and encouraged the brothers (emphasis added).

And in Romans 16:3 and 5, Paul exhorts his readers to "Greet Prisca and Aquila, my co-workers in Christ Jesus . . . greet also the church *at their house*."

And though the *ekklesia* was not yet established during Jesus' ministry on earth, He met with His disciples on boats, on hillsides, and on the shores of the Sea of Galilee—wherever it was necessary to share with people about the kingdom of God. He modeled meeting with people wherever necessary to teach them about the kingdom of God! Is it in a prison? A movie theater? A hotel conference room?

The type of structure people gather in, the schedule of service, and the time of meeting should always be secondary over people gathering together to worship the Lord Jesus Christ! What is most important is bringing Jesus to unreached people, not trying to bring them to church. And sometimes this means taking unreasonable steps—including taking on a missionary mindset and letting creative juices flow!

REACHING OUT TO MILLENNIALS

Planted in 2007, Experience Life is a non-denominational church in Lubbock, Texas. The church began meeting in a rented skating rink, not in a school, because there were rules against allowing churches to meet at local schools. When Pastor Chris Galanos and his wife came to start the church in their hometown after graduating from seminary, they sent out letters asking for support because they didn't have a sending church. One generous couple called and told Pastor Chris that they would cover his family's living expenses for two years, giving him the opportunity to focus on launching the new church.

The group began praying, planning and gathering people to help them plant the church. Pastor Chris encouraged their core group to pray for 10,000 people to be saved in ten years. Experience Life Church now has around 4,000 people meeting in five locations. One of their locations meets on the campus of Texas Tech University. The university church site is called Raider Church after the school's nickname, the Red Raiders.

With Chris as lead pastor and Clayton Walker as the executive pastor, most of their congregation consists of millennials and their children. More than 60 percent of the young adults attending Experience Life have not previously attended church anywhere. The church faces particular challenges in finding Christian leaders to lead small groups.

As a young man, Pastor Chris had a passion and gift for working with computers. His dad prayed that he would have the same passion and drive for Christ as he had for computers and God answered his father's prayer. Chris was involved in the college age ministry of his church and decided to pursue ministry instead of taking a lucrative career path in technology. Perhaps seeing his dad's example of faith and prayer led Chris and the pastors at Experience Life Church to emphasize prayer as a key element in the life and growth of the church.

Experience Life is characterized by a deep commitment to prayer. Each campus gathers the staff to meet weekly for prayer and worship. The Experience Life website notes about the weekly prayer gathering: *"If we want to see results like they saw in the Book of Acts, we have to pray like they prayed in the Book of Acts."* Committed to a ministry of prayer, the early Christians saw God working, and so must Christians be equally committed to prayer today.

FINDING A MODEL THAT WORKS

When Experience Life Church began, the church was meeting weekly in homes as small groups. It wasn't their intention to change that plan. Pastor Chris was passionately committed to the cell-church model and believed it was the way they needed to go, but the church was exploding in the weekend gatherings. On the first day the church launched, 300 people came, and they went up to 1,000 within a year. As the weekend crowds grew quickly, they had to reconsider their model. They adjusted their plan, believing that bringing the gospel to all who would hear was more important than the model.

They concluded that God didn't call them to a model or a form. God called them to make disciples, and they believed that whatever was working (for example, these weekend gatherings which were so well attended) was where they needed to be. At that point, they started launching new church locations in rented buildings. They were more committed to Jesus' mission to reach the lost than the cell-church model.

While Experience Life was working through these adjustments, they began addressing the fact that many students at Texas Tech were not in church *anywhere*. Often, many high school students attend church before going to college but a huge percentage of them stop going when they start college. Ray Comfort, Founder and CEO of Living Waters (a ministry that inspires and equips Christians to fulfill the Great Commission), writes that 80 percent of youth leave church after high school! Comfort says, "As a parent, that's the most horrifying statistic in the world to me! Let me bring that closer to home. That means, in a church youth group with 20 kids, over 15 will no longer go to church after they graduate. In a home, three out of four of our kids statistically will forsake fellowship by the time they're 18. The cry of all of our hearts should be "Why?"[4]

Some students admit they want a break from church, but most say they are simply too busy, or it's not convenient to get to. And the sad truth is many have never crossed over from darkness to life. Many are simply not saved to begin with.

Texas Tech had over 35,000 students. Experience Life realized it had an unreached people group right in its backyard. Their members began to pray and prepare to reach out on the Red Raiders campus. How could they effectively reach out to the Tech students?

RAIDER CHURCH

Church ministry to young adults is a tricky business, as any church in a college town knows. Experience Life evaluated their existing ministries to college students

4 http://www.onthebox.us/2013/01/words-of-comfort-why-do-80-of-youth.html

and studied the church structures and environments. None of them were focused on plugging students into Experience Life as it was. So instead of trying to bring the students to the church, they decided to make something new. They would bring the church to the students. Experience Life made the decision to plant a church on Texas Tech's campus.

When Raider Church began, it started at a church site close to the college campus, and 500 students came the first night to a building that only seated 400. With standing room only, the unique church launch quickly outgrew that facility and moved to its second iteration. They went to a bigger church site campus, which was quite far away from Texas Tech. That night the church had 700 in attendance. Within just a few weeks the leadership team realized that many of the Tech students would never be able to go to a site so far away.

Immediately they went back to the Tech campus and rented a university auditorium, where the young start-up church has about 1,000 students in attendance. The location was a key component for Raider Church. Because they are located on the Texas Tech campus, most of the students can even walk to their service.

But starting a church on a state-funded college campus meant that many typical church processes and models had to be tossed out. Experience Life was comfortable in breaking the mold, but they had to break it even more to launch this church of college students. The Experience Life leadership team asked, "What would work?" instead of "What has been done?"

Experience Life, like other multi-site churches, had mastered the technology and logistics of broadcasting teaching to other sites. The other Experience Life sites would receive the same messages by the same pastor each weekend, keeping the church united and connected. With Raider Church, the leadership team presented the entire service live, with an in-person speaker. Since the church asked "What would work?" they found that the students were more drawn to an entirely live service rather than sermons streamed on a screen.

The calendar of events at Raider Church is also unique. The leaders learned to work with the ebb and flow of the college schedule, rather than work against it. Instead of meeting on weekends, the church meets at 9:00 p.m. on Tuesday nights. Executive Pastor Clayton teaches weekly at Raider Church, with teaching geared for the students.

MOVING FORWARD UNDER GOD'S LEADERSHIP

It can be difficult to define success in a ministry to an ever-changing group of young college students, but Experience Life is focused on new believers and mature disciples.

Raider Church is the result of a missionary mindset. Pastor Clayton says that, "Even in America, we've got to live and think like missionaries." As a result of its ministry to college students, Experience Life has also focused on developing young leaders. The church created a school and discipleship ministry for upcoming leaders called Protégé. The church hired a full-time director of the program, and the training develops the young leaders in 12 to 18 months.

As prayer is a continued focus of the church, all of their expansions and launches have been flooded with prayer. Among many specifically answered prayers, 500 were saved on Easter Sunday, there were over 600 baptisms over a two-week event, and the Raider Church has continued reaching out to the Texas Tech students. In one instance, when church equipment had been stolen, the church prayed during the service that God would convict the thieves to return the stolen equipment. About two weeks later, the thieves repented and returned the church's property.

Experience Life is still praying for ten campuses in ten years, and God has continued to bless them. The church has been able to add a new location every year. Students like Jeremy have had the church brought to them.

UN**REASONABLE** CHURCHES

QUESTIONS TO CONSIDER

- What is your church doing to reach the next generation?

- Are there areas where your church may be stuck in the cycle of 'what has been done', rather than 'what will work'?

- What would need to change to break out of that cycle?

TAKEAWAY POINTS TO ACT ON:

1. *Are you living and thinking like a missionary?* Like it or not, there are unreached people groups right in our backyards. What can you do to adjust your thinking and methodologies? Having a missionary mindset means adjusting ourselves for the sake of others; to change what we need to change and do what we need to do. We need to look around and see who the unreached people are in our neighborhoods, praying and seeking God to give us the wisdom and passion for the lost.

2. *Are you training a new generation of leaders?* New leaders are the lifeblood of the church. Every generation needs them. Is your church looking for and training new leaders to take on new ministries?

3. *Do you believe in prayer?* The leaders at Experience Life teach that seeking the Lord is greater than models or strategies. Rather than replicating what other churches are doing, are you praying that God's will be done? Are you teaching church members to pray in services where people can confess, seek God, and worship Him?

4. *In trying to reach young adults, are you where they are?* Raider Church is unique in many ways, but it's not that different than many mission churches around the world. Those who can lead and teach the gospel need to go to unreasonable locations where the people are. People aren't going to just come to a church. The church has to come to them.

5. *Finding a schedule that works might be the best way to reach millennials.* Raider Church meets at 9:00 p.m. on Tuesday nights. The world is a different place than it was 20 years ago. Sunday is not a protected day anymore in our culture. Be creative with the missionary mindset.

6. *Multi-site doesn't necessarily mean "clone church."* The Raider Church story is refreshing because it shows that multi-site churches aren't always best served by "cloning" the mother church. How are the people at the other church site being served and challenged in their unique situation?

Chapter 7

UNREASONABLE FOCUS

ATOURIST VISITING AUSTRALIA was so engrossed in her phone's Facebook feed that she walked off the edge of a pier into the frigid waters of Port Phillip Bay. The hapless woman didn't know how to swim, but was quickly rescued and taken to a hospital. Even though her ordeal could have been deadly in the freezing water, she remained steadfast and focused: she didn't even lose her phone.

There is so much talk about what a church should be focused on. Should we be focused on evangelism or discipleship? Perhaps churches are too intently focused on one or the other to see the big picture. An *unreasonable* church does the hard work of both saving the lost and discipling the saved.

COMMISSION TO DISCIPLESHIP

Jerry Root, associate director of the Institute for Strategic Evangelism at Wheaton College, says asking why evangelism and discipleship should work hand in hand is like asking, "What came first, the chicken or the egg?"

What should be considered is what Jesus commissioned the disciples to do in those moments before He ascended to heaven to the Father:

> Then Jesus came to them and said, "All authority in heaven and on earth has been given to me. Therefore go and make disciples of all nations, baptizing them in the name of the Father and of the Son and of the Holy Spirit, and teaching them to obey everything I have commanded you. And surely I am with you always, to the very end of the age."
>
> – MATTHEW 28:18–20 NIV, EMPHASIS ADDED

Jesus left His disciples with these last and profound words before leaving this earth, communicating how things should be done when He was no longer with them in the flesh. He commanded them to evangelize in order to make more disciples. He never said, "Go and make more converts!"

There is a precise order in Jesus' directive! Disciples evangelize to produce more disciples.

Mark's gospel reveals this order in Jesus' calling of the first disciples:

> Afterward Jesus went up on a mountain and called out the ones he wanted to go with him. And they came to him. Then he appointed twelve of them and called them his apostles. They were to accompany him, and *he would send them out to preach.*
>
> – MARK 3:13–14 NLT, EMPHASIS ADDED

Looking over the few years Jesus spent with His disciples before His death, it is clear that Jesus poured into their lives, molding and shaping their unique personalities for the task ahead. Jesus' end goal for each disciple was that they would be active and effective in ministry to be able to go out when He was no longer present with them, and make more disciples (who would make more disciples). Discipleship came before evangelism, but evangelism lead immediately into discipleship.

Notice too the order of what those disciples were called in the Bible. Prior to Jesus' death, burial and resurrection, Scripture refers to those twelve followers as "disciples," which means "learners." After His resurrection, Scripture refers to them as "apostles," or "sent ones." Were they, as Mary Poppins said, "practically perfect in every way?" By no means! But they were in the process of maturing to be more and more like Christ each day. This is the only requirement of an apostle! And a believer never stops being one or the other— they are continually both: they are students of the Lord Jesus Christ who are also His ambassadors on earth.

In John 8:31–32 Jesus says, "To the Jews who had believed him, Jesus said, "If you hold to my teaching, you are really my disciples. Then you will know the truth, and the truth will set you free." Once a person experiences salvation, there is an immediate responsibility—to hold to Jesus' teachings in the Word of God. This is discipleship, and only then will people experience true freedom!

SEEKING THE LOST *AND* THE SAVED

Christ Community Church was started in 1984 by six couples in St. Charles, Illinois, who wanted a church for their friends and neighbors. They prayed together and hired a young pastor named Jim Nicodem. Jim and his wife have served Christ Community for thirty years and are still going strong.

Christ Community now meets in four locations and has an attendance of 5,000 people each week in the western suburbs of Chicago. The church meets at the Bartlett Campus, Blackberry Creek Campus, DeKalb Campus, and the St. Charles Campus. The church's mission is to make "passionate disciples of Jesus Christ, who are belonging, growing, serving and reaching."

From the beginning, the church sought to be a church that reached "seekers" (whom they now call "explorers"). Christ Community wanted to cast a wide net to appeal to the spiritually lost. Back in the day when the "seeker sensitive" church was a relatively new idea, Pastor Jim was connected with Bill Hybels, who planted Willow Creek and was certainly a pioneer of the seeker friendly concept.

But this methodology has had many legitimate criticisms. To go "wide" meant that the church could not go "deep," according to many voices. During the time that Christ Community began, American churches began to be separated by an ideological divide. On one side, the attractional or "seeker sensitive" churches claimed their mission was to reach the unchurched and unchristian. On the other side, the discipleship-based churches maintained that their primary focus should be toward existing Christians. In other words, the focus became either evangelism or discipleship. This issue has continued to divide American Christianity.

Pastor Jim struggled with these issues. He desperately wanted to reach the lost but also saw the problems of "easy-believism." After reading Scot McKnight's book *The King Jesus Gospel*, Pastor Jim thought the author's attempt to deal with the "wide" church drifted too close to works-based righteousness. As a faithful student of the Bible, the pastor studied the Scriptures' heartbeat: the gospel promises. He realized that there could be a better way than landing on one side or other of the seeker/Christian divide.

From its earliest days, Pastor Jim and Christ Community saw the deep flaws in this either/or debate. If a church was only focused on evangelism, the trade-off was spiritual growth and maturity. If the church was only focused on discipleship, the trade-off was the unchurched being unreached.

Pastor Jim wanted to balance the division between evangelism churches and discipleship churches. He wanted to go "deep" as well as "wide."

GOING DEEP AND WIDE

Pastor Jim has a passion for reaching lost people and a passion for digging deeper into theological teaching; he is passionate about going after the lost, and also leading them to be disciples who are taught the deep truths of Scripture. Christ Community Church decided to bring attractional and discipleship-based ministry together on their church campuses, reaching lost people and bringing theologically sound teaching to them.

To bring the two approaches together in a unified focus, the church reaches "wide" with attractional events and outreaches, but also "deep" with an intentional plan to bring new Christians to spiritual maturity.

Going Deep in Evangelism

Pastor Jim and his staff have intentionally reworked their evangelistic materials to build disciples, not just count decisions. The materials emphasize Biblical texts and concepts such as salvation by grace through faith (Eph.2:8–9), but also continues with Ephesians 2:10; that God has created us in Christ Jesus to do good works, which He prepared in advance for us. It's not just an attempt at casting a wide net to get people saved, but instead a focus on a deep and wide net. Salvation means intentionally living life according to God's plans and purposes.

Going Deep in Preaching

Pastor Jim recognizes that the seeker-focused or Christian-focused churches usually have different preaching styles. Topically based sermons tend to be more accessible and attractive to those who haven't grown up in the church, while verse by verse exposition teaches Biblical literacy and understanding. Again, instead of being "either/or," Pastor Jim takes a "both/ and" approach to preaching. His sermons are mostly topical, but he packages the topics within a particular passage of Scripture. With a D. Min with an emphasis on hermeneutics from Trinity Evangelical, Pastor Jim is conscious of working to interpret the topic in light of Scripture rather than the other way around.

So, much topical preaching is about choosing a topic and then working in various verses cherry-picked to support it, but Pastor Jim intentionally teaches his topical sermons from one passage. Pastor Jim's topical sermons take up about 80 percent of his preaching, but he also spends time working exegetically through larger chunks. His goal is to teach the congregation how to work through a segment of Scripture, so they learn how to work through the Scriptures themselves. A few times a year he will walk through large segments of Scripture, but will give each sermon a topical title.

Going Deep in Worship

Many attractional churches tend to be very high energy in their worship services, and that was also true of Christ Community Church for many years. However, Pastor Jim found himself drawn to evangelical churches with a more liturgical style when he had Sundays off. He thought carefully about why he was attracted to those churches.

In those liturgical services, there was often the recitation of creeds, times of silence, prayer and confession, and Scripture that was read out loud in responsive, congregational styles. Pastor Jim looked at how Pastor Glenn Packiam was presenting modern music with a liturgical style at the New Life Church in Colorado Springs, Colorado. Pastor Glenn believes that the music of the church should not just be a faith-expressing activity, but also a profoundly faith-shaping activity.

Pastor Glenn's thoughts helped Christ Community understand their focus as they sought to blend liturgical ideas with modern music. Grasping the idea that worship was also a time for confession and teaching, the church added a teaching pastor to the worship teams. At first, this threw off the worship team, but they learned how to work with a pastor who was tasked with driving the worship music from a teaching, faith-shaping perspective. The teaching pastor began screening out songs with no theological value and added songs that helped move the teaching themes along; other liturgical elements were added, such as silence and confessional prayer.

Going Deep in Community Groups

Bringing together the potentially difficult focus points of "deep" and "wide" meant an understanding of where people were at as they came into the fellowship. The first few steps of connecting people into small groups are intentionally designed. Christ Community has three different "on-ramps," depending on where the newcomers were starting. For those "explorers" who are just beginning to investigate, the on ramp is a small group class called *Alpha*.

For the new believers, the on-ramp is a course called *Next Steps*. For Christians who have transferred from another church, their on-ramp is a seminar entitled *Begin to Belong*. The on-ramps are designed to move people forward in their journey to an ongoing community group. These small groups are intentionally focused on Bible study, using carefully curated materials. The community groups encourage personal Bible reading and discussion of Biblical passages.

Pastor Jim wrote a four-book collection published by Moody called *Bible Savvy*. The books are used as training material for small group leaders and study material for many of the groups. Starting from the basic story of the Bible and moving to more complex issues of apologetics and hermeneutics, the series helps the Christian apply Biblical truth.

The Results of Going Deep and Wide

Christ Community is developing both better biblical literacy and discipleship among its members and is continuing to be effective in its evangelistic outreach to the community. In 2015, during the December outreach services, 170 people came forward to pick up their Next Step Packet, showing their desire to follow Christ. These new Christians were encouraged and supported by their respective campus ministries.

By having an intentional way to follow up on and direct new members to the right "on-ramp," the church takes care to make sure the wide net helps those they catch to go deep. Their plans are working well, as they see 75% to 80% of their weekend attendees involved with the ongoing community groups.

As Jerry Root writes:

> "Evangelism begins and ends in discipleship. Perhaps 'ends' is an inappropriate word, for the ministry of Christ in the world is ongoing. God grants to each generation both the responsibility and privilege of serving his purposes. To be a disciple of Christ is to know the love and calling of God and to assume the responsibility to tell others that they are deeply loved and forgiven by God."

The tourist visiting Australia was so caught up in what she was focused on that she fell off the end of a pier. Focusing on breadth, only reaching others for Christ, without feeding believers by going deep, will leave both sides sinking.

QUESTIONS TO CONSIDER

- Are you building an organization, or growing disciples?

- Is your church focused too heavily on one area—evangelism or discipleship?

- What would it take to balance leadership efforts in both areas? What would have to change?

- Will many churches find that they have plunged off the pier when the Day of Accountability comes for church leaders?

TAKEAWAY POINTS TO ACT ON:

1. *Attractional churches can help make disciples with good preaching.* Topics can be taught packaged in a scriptural text. Expository teaching helps build understanding in a coherent way. Too often, churches don't teach Scripture in its entire context. Christ Community is leading the way in bringing the timeless Word to an ever-changing world. They are training their members to read the Word of God in context for the meaning God intended rather than using the Bible like a pile of fortune cookies.

2. *Worship is about shaping faith, not just expressing faith.* What will your church learn from the music at your church? Will they learn about Jesus and being justified by faith, or will they say "Jesus, I love you" 70 times? Would a seeker benefit from that? Use this time wisely! Strengthen and shape their growing faith by intentional faith building aspects like theologically sound lyrics, times for confessional prayer and contemplation, Scripture reading and other liturgical forms.

3. *Help new people know which on-ramp is right for them.* Keep the options simple and direct. Guiding new people to the right connections and small groups is crucial to growing a church both wide and deep.

4. *Be discerning about materials that are used for small groups.* Consider using Christ Community's curriculum or creating your own basic, foundational teaching materials. Pastor Jim's Bible Savvy book series can be found at this link: http://amzn.to/1Y3Zm0H

5. *Leaders lead by example.* If you want your church members to be in small groups, then you need to be in a small group yourself. Pastor Jim has always been in a community group, often with one or two members who are not Christians. Instead of twisting arms

a few times a year, a pastor in a community group can continually share his experiences.

6. *Keep it simple.* Churches are notorious for crazy amounts of programs and classes. Christ Community asks four things of their church members:

- Attend a weekend service.

- Serve in some way.

- Be in a community group.

- Once a year, receive some training (short classes offered in marriage, parenting, Bible understanding, evangelism, etc.)

Chapter 8:

UNREASONABLE DIVERSITY

GATHERED IN THE locker room before the final game of the year, each of the players considers his role on the team. This is the biggest game. This is the game that will determine if the team is considered a winner or the first loser. This is the goal of the season. Suddenly, the quarterback stands up and says to the coach: "Um, coach, I don't really feel like you understand me. I mean, you're black and I'm white, and well, I think that maybe we need a coach that I can identify with better, you know. I think I should go play for another team that I can feel more comfortable with."

These are not the words of a player who is there to win. These are the words of a player who is focused on something else than the team's goal and purpose. The church of Jesus Christ is glued together by a greater goal than gathering people who look alike in a building. The church has a Great Commission: Go into all the ethnos (which means ethnic groups) and make disciples. The Great Commission is not just about going across the sea to evangelize, but going across the street to love all (ethnic) neighbors. In a day when racial divides are still one of the greatest worldwide struggles, the *unreasonable* church is turning us back toward the church's mission.

COMING TOGETHER IN CHRIST

The church in Antioch, described in the Book of Acts, is a model for ethnically diverse churches today. This fledgling church focused on the gospel rather than consumer-based growth strategies. In its infancy, the early church experienced great diversity—not only with different races but also with cultures, languages, and classes.

The beginning of Acts 13 displays this difference, even amongst the leaders:

> Now in the church at Antioch there were prophets and teachers: Barnabas, Simeon called Niger, Lucius of Cyrene, Manaen (who had been brought up with Herod the tetrarch) and Saul.
>
> – ACTS 13:1

The Antioch church leaders were diverse. Barnabas was a Jewish man—a teacher and evangelist sent by the church based out of Jerusalem to care for the Antiochan church. Paul identifies Simeon as Niger, which is the country next to the African Niger River. Lucius is of Cyrene—or North Africa (west of Egypt). Each came from different backgrounds and from different cultures and classes. But in Christ they are brothers, ministering together for the sake of the gospel.

Paul reminds us that ethnic, religious, cultural, or language barriers—and even age and gender barriers—should never stop a church from reaching a particular group of people. As believers in Christ, *all* are part of the family of God—and the church should reflect this! Recall what Paul says regarding what happens when diverse people come together in Christ:

> Remember that at that time you were separate from Christ, excluded from citizenship in Israel and foreigners to the covenants of the promise, without hope and without God in the world. But now in Christ Jesus you who once were far away have been brought near by the blood of Christ. For he himself is our peace, who has made the two groups one and has destroyed the barrier, the dividing wall of hostility.
> – EPHESIANS 2:12–14 NIV

A DIVERSE CHURCH

Transformation Church is a multi-ethnic, multi-generational church led by Pastor Derwin Gray. The fellowship was launched in February 2010 by Pastor Gray, his wife, and a few others. At their first service, they had 701 people in attendance and have grown to 3,000 with four campuses, including two located in prisons.

From the beginning, the church wanted to create a more unified and integrated church. The focus remains an embodying of the gospel, which Pastor Gray describes as "the rule and reign of Jesus," through ethnic reconciliation and social economic justice. The church attempts to reach out to all ethnicities in their neighborhood and especially minister to the poor. Pastor Gray says they are more concerned about ministry than typical church growth metrics. They care more about their impact in the community than being recognized as one of the fastest growing churches in the United States.

Pastor Gray and his wife met each other as students at Brigham Young University, where they attended as non-Mormons and non-Christians. He was a talented football player and had the opportunity to play for the Indianapolis Colts in the NFL. During his first year in the NFL, a teammate introduced him to the Christian faith. Around the same time, his wife heard the gospel from a co-worker. They both came to faith in 1997. Shortly after, they moved to Charlotte, North Carolina so that he could play for the Carolina Panthers.

The next year or so became a time of questions and searching as the new Christians encountered an essential issue that created the foundation of Transformation Church.

DON'T CRITICIZE—*CREATE!*

As a Christian NFL player, Pastor Gray began to speak at youth events and churches. Neither he nor his wife had grown up in church, and these speaking engagements were their first experiences with a wide variety of churches. He was overwhelmed to find that churches were deeply segregated. The church was the least diverse environment he had ever experienced. He recalled being in night clubs and seeing all kinds of people, but when it came to churches, there were black churches and there were white churches. Few churches had a representation of multiple ethnicities. Churches are ten times more segregated than the local schools they are near and twenty times more segregated than their neighborhoods.

As a new Christian, he searched the Bible for answers to this dilemma. He didn't find any discussion of black or white churches in the Bible, but he discovered the great divide between Jewish and Gentile Christians in the New Testament. As he studied more, he saw the racism and the "hurricane of violence" of the ancient world; but positioned right in the very center of the storm was the New Testament church, made up of both Jews and Gentiles. The church was making unified friends and co-laborers out of former enemies.

The gospel of Jesus Christ brought about reconciliation between vastly different people:

> For as many of you as were baptized into Christ have put on Christ. There is neither Jew nor Greek, there is neither slave nor free, there is no male and female, for you are all one in Christ Jesus. And if you are Christ's, then you are Abraham's offspring, heirs according to promise.
>
> – GALATIANS 3:27-29 ESV

Pastor Gray began to ask church leaders about the stark lack of diversity. If the New Testament demonstrated the unity of Jews and Gentiles, why is segregation such an embedded part of churches today? Time after time, he received responses that he thought were inadequate and horrible. As he struggled with these answers, he was convicted that rather than criticizing, he needed to create. Transformation Church began out of a desire to see the church minister to all people.

A GOSPEL FOCUS

Pastor Gray is not afraid to buck the trends of modern American Christianity. New church plants often have a "target" demographic in mind: a certain neighborhood or even social status of people to go after. Transformation Church believes that this "targeted audience" model itself can create church segregation. The purpose of reaching the demographic becomes stronger than reaching the lost with the gospel. Trying to hit the target audience, churches often hire staff who, "look" like the target, and so the gospel outreach to all people is easily lost in the shuffle.

Pastor Gray is not a fan of churches with a consumer mentality. When people are looking to "buy" the look and feel (the brand) of the church and the leadership cultivates that mindset, the church culture becomes self-seeking, without the glue necessary to hold a diverse church body together. Indeed, "contextualization" is a buzzword in the American church, with a focus on relating the church ministry and message to the culture of the target demographic. Pastor Gray believes this is backward. Churches built on this kind of framework may find that church attendees may not be willing to stick around in a specifically contextualized church as culture is an ever changing, fluid concept.

Studying the Book of Acts, Pastor Gray saw the glue that held ethnically divided churches together; it was not a demographic study or consumer-based church growth strategies. The glue that held the New Testament church together was the gospel itself, with all of its implications.

At Transformation Church, the gospel is front and center in everything that they do. Their church culture is based on the implications of the gospel, lived out in these ways:

1. By the reconciliation with God, that comes through Christ's finished work on the cross.

2. By the reconciliation and peace with people, that comes from a new life in Christ.

Reconciliation is the result of gospel transformation. When Christians are united with God, they are united with each other. In Pastor Gray's vision to "create" instead of criticizing, he was convicted that the church needs to have "cross-eyed" leaders, envisioning the gospel's effect on our relationship with God and others.

This is the goal of Transformation Church—to keep the whole story of the gospel in front of the believer. Rather than a social event or a "get out of hell free" card, Pastor Gray teaches that the body of Christ, covered by the righteousness of Christ, is meant to be a foretaste of the new heaven and earth that God will create at Christ's return. And the vision of the Book of Revelation presents a multitude from every tribe, tongue, and nation, unified by its worship of the Lamb. As God's kingdom to come is, in a sense, already here, Christians should be displaying kingdom characteristics.

UPWARD, INWARD, OUTWARD

Transformation Church baptized nearly 400 people in 2015, and continues to be one of the fastest growing churches in the country, but Pastor Gray bristles at the ratings on numbers. His concern is that the culture of evangelical churches is focused on the wrong metrics: "budgets, buildings, and butts." Transformation Church wants to see churches serve their communities and trust God for the results. As Transformation now has campuses in local prisons and has adopted four schools, the gospel implications continue to flow from the congregation. The word many use to describe Transformation Church is, "Loving." Pastor Gray will take that description any day over "hip" or "trendy".

At the end of every service, the church repeats their mission statement together out loud:

- Upward: We love God completely.

- Inward: We love ourselves correctly.

- Outward: We love our neighbors compassionately.

The church's mission is the gospel, and the gospel is the unifying goal. Pastor Gray compares the focus of winning in sports with the church. The team is motivated and unified by the desire to win the game. The players don't say to the coach, "You don't look like me, and I can't relate to you, so I'm going to another team where I can feel comfortable." Likewise, the coach doesn't tell the team owner that he doesn't want the star player from Iowa on his team because he's used to New Yorkers; more important things hold the team together.

Transformation Church is held together by its members' common love for God, their identity in Christ, and their love for their neighbors. Barriers come down, and differences fade. Pastor Gray saw the glue that held ethnically divided churches together was not a demographic study or consumer-based church growth strategies. The glue that held the New Testament church together was the gospel itself, with all of its implications.

QUESTIONS TO CONSIDER

- What is holding your church together?
- Does your church meet the needs of the different cultural, ethnic, and generational groups in your community?
- In what ways is your church possibly giving in to a "consumer mentality"?
- How is this possibly impacting the dynamics between church members?

TAKEAWAY POINTS TO ACT ON:

1. *Is your church driven by theological conviction, or social pressure?* When coaching other pastors on how to better integrate their churches, Pastor Gray instructs them that it must be founded on a theological conviction, not cultural relevance. Our motives should be based on the true gospel where Jesus is the superglue that unites former enemies so we can reflect God's glory. Transform your church into a foretaste of the kingdom to come, where ethnic differences don't separate people.

2. *An "integrated" church won't happen by just changing the faces up front.* Sin blinds selfish people to those around them. Hiring fresh

faces that look "different" will not in itself inspire integration. Once you change your view of the gospel, grounding yourself in God's Word and teaching it to your congregation, then you may move out to make your staff and leadership more ethnically diverse, but the first move is to make sure your mind and heart are following God's heart.

3. *Embrace the implications of the gospel.* Says Pastor Gray: "The gospel is more than "I get to go to Heaven when I die." The gospel is a royal announcement that through Jesus' life, death, resurrection, ascension, and sending of the Spirit, a church has been formed to be a foretaste of the kingdom to come. And that church is Jews and Gentiles who've been reconciled through the body of Christ that as Ephesians 2:14 says is a new humanity, and this humanity is a multiethnic humanity.

4. *Are "budgets, buildings, and butts" your metrics for growth?* It's so easy to get caught up in these statistics, and they are used to measure the value of churches today. As Pastor Gray says, "even weeds grow fast." What is applauded is what gets done. Perhaps the church should be asking whose applause we should be seeking.

5. *Has Pastor Gray caught on to one of the secrets for reaching millennials?* Many church leaders are puzzling over the difficulties reaching the new generation of emerging adults, with all the complexities of their culture. Young adults experience schools, neighborhoods, and their local hangouts as incredibly diverse, but churches are typically segregated. Could culturally diverse churches be a key to winning the younger generation?

6. *Read about Pastor Gray's vision to inspire church leaders.* His book is entitled, *The High Definition Leader: Building Multiethnic Churches in a Multiethnic World* and can be found at this link: http://amzn.to/2blUDYY

Chapter 9

UNREASONABLE EXPANSION

THE FIRST QUINTUPLETS known to have survived infancy were born on May 28, 1934 near the village of Corbeil in Ontario, Canada. The five daughters were born in a farmhouse and kept warm in wicker laundry baskets borrowed from neighbors. After a few months with their parents, the five girls were made wards of the government of Ontario, who built a house for the quintuplets that became a tourist attraction.

From 1936 to 1943, around 3,000,000 people visited the observation gallery of the outdoor playground. The tourist trap was called "Quintland" and became the biggest attraction in Ontario, visited even more than the Canadian side of Niagara Falls. The Dionne Quintuplets became one of the biggest stories of the Depression Era.

People flock to see the new and different. In the late 1930s, no one had ever heard of quintuplets. As the North American church growth movement has exploded in the last 25 years, many churches have been "birthed." But who would give birth to "church quintuplets?" It's the *unreasonable* church that launches five infant churches at once.

WISE STEWARDS

It doesn't matter how many campus start-ups a church desires to plant; it must be done by the Lord's leading and with the right motives. Church start-ups for the sake of numbers mean nothing in God's economy. However, the church featured in this chapter, 12Stone, realized an important biblical principal related to stewardship of God's money and experienced the results of walking in obedience to God's instruction. This principle can be found in Jesus' Parable of the Talents:

> For it will be like a man going on a journey, who called his servants and entrusted to them his property. To one he gave five talents, to another two, to another one, to each according to his ability. Then he went away. He who had received the five talents went at once and traded with them, and he made five talents more. So also he who had the two talents made two talents more. But he who had received the one talent went and dug in the ground and hid his master's money. Now after a long time the master of those servants came and settled accounts with them. And he who had received the five talents came forward, bringing five talents more, saying, 'Master, you delivered to me five talents; here I have made five talents more.' His master said to him, 'Well done, good and faithful servant. You have been faithful over a little; I will

set you over much. Enter into the joy of your master.' And he also who had the two talents came forward, saying, 'Master, you delivered to me two talents; here I have made two talents more.' His master said to him, 'Well done, good and faithful servant. You have been faithful over a little; I will set you over much. Enter into the joy of your master.' He also who had received the one talent came forward, saying, 'Master, I knew you to be a hard man, reaping where you did not sow, and gathering where you scattered no seed, so I was afraid, and I went and hid your talent in the ground. Here you have what is yours.' But his master answered him, 'You wicked and slothful servant! You knew that I reap where I have not sown and gather where I scattered no seed? Then you ought to have invested my money with the bankers, and at my coming I should have received what was my own with interest. So take the talent from him and give it to him who has the ten talents. For to everyone who has will more be given, and he will have an abundance. But from the one who has not, even what he has will be taken away.

– MATTHEW 25:14–29

An ancient unit of measure used universally in Rome, the Middle East, and Greece was a "talent"—the value of money, or a coin. In this parable, Jesus was referring to the largest unit of currency at the time. In this parable, Jesus takes notice of the faithful servant who is wise with the money his master entrusted to him.

The Parable of the Talents says to wise stewards of God's money, "Because you have been faithful over little; I will set you over much" (Matt. 25:23), and "For everyone who has will more be given and he will have an abundance" (Matt. 25:29). 12Stone realized the benefit of launching multiple campuses—the saving of millions of dollars, both in facilities and in raising leaders to take on these new campuses.

SLOW GROWTH TO STAGGERING GROWTH

Pastor Kevin Myers and a small core group launched 12Stone Church in Atlanta, Georgia in 1987. The church is a congregation of the Wesleyan Church and aligned with the ministry style of the Willow Creek Association. It took seven years for the church to grow to 200 members, and 14 more years before it grew to 1,500 attendees. Before their latest launch, the church met at four campuses with around 20,000 members. In 2010, Outreach Magazine named 12Stone the number one fastest growing church in America.

The church's DNA is centered in three components: Spiritual intensity, creative ideation, and leadership development. They are concerned for *the lost* (they will do anything to reach them), *the least* (they want to give themselves away and serve them), and *leadership* (raising the next generation to be leaders).

Since 2007, when the church took on the 12Stone

name, a reference to the 12 stones of remembrance that Joshua and the Israelites set up when they crossed the Jordan River, 12Stone's blistering growth pace has been fueled by the launches of multiple church sites. In each of the first few launches, they aimed for 350 attendees but quickly found that 750 was a better estimate at the number of seats needed for the new church start-ups.

As they evaluated their next move from four campuses toward more growth, they knew that it was time to launch more campuses. They began working out the logistics of new locations. A new location always meant growth from momentum. When a new site was launched, newcomers came in waves. But they also wanted the members at all four campuses to be affected. They didn't want the new start-ups to be a side event in the church's life where just a handful of members were active. They wanted investment from the entire church at the various sites, even though all would feel the loss of members at the home site as a result of the launch. Could new launches inspire less active members to step up and volunteer for the responsibilities left vacant because of the launch?

During this time of discovery, they realized that starting more than one campus at a time saved money. The church learned from the earlier site launches that they could launch multiple campuses for millions of dollars less than starting just one. The new sites each had a three-phase growth plan. Phase one would be a temporary rented facility. Phase two would be to grow the campus and maximize the rented facility. And the third phase would be to seek 24/7 buildings for ministry, whether a long term lease or physically building from the ground up. Working multiple launches together would be good stewardship of church resources.

In a similar way, teamwork was a significant consideration. If the church launched more than one campus at a time, the campus pastors, worship leaders, and staff could train together, encourage each other, and learn together as they launched. This planning and preparation was guided along by Pastor Myers' vision to launch five church sites in the next five years.

CHURCH PIONEERS STEP UP

As a result of this planning and preparation, 12Stone prayerfully decided to do the unreasonable: they would launch five new campuses simultaneously, increasing their total number of campuses to nine. They spent nearly two years praying and preparing for the launch. Primarily, the planning involved the mobilization of five sets of pastors and staff for the five launches. Raising leaders was always at the heart of 12Stone's culture, so they already had three available campus ministers from within the church. Two more campus pastors were sought from a network of churches familiar to 12Stone.

Preparation also meant replacing the many leaders and volunteers who would be moving from existing church sites to the new launches. 1,700 adults were moving to the new campuses, many of who were leaders and high-level volunteers. To replace that many people, 12Stone emphasized that this was a "pioneer" movement for the entire church. Some of the "pioneers" were leaving for the new start-ups, but the "sending pioneers" needed to fill the gaps that were left behind. They encouraged the "senders" to step up and serve. They created "Step Up" t-shirts and "Step Up" events to encourage their members and make it fun.

The "pioneer" movement was an investment for all the existing 12Stone members at the various campuses. They kept open communication with the existing campuses about how all of the pieces of the puzzle were coming together for the five launches. They encouraged congregational input, questions, and prayer.

Finding five adequate sites to rent for the launching churches was one of the most complicated matters of the planning. Many church members were involved in the search. As the church shared its need to find more options to look into, church members would suggest potential meeting sites. The leadership team made a list of 400 sites to investigate as possible meeting locations. In one area they found that a third of the schools weren't interested in working with them, a third already had churches meeting there, and a third just wouldn't work because of the facilities. They were even barred from renting an empty grocery store because of the county's concerns about having a church in that location. Creative ideation kept them adjusting and moving on in their plans. However, finding locations for all five of their launches at once was certainly the most complex issue for the "Pioneer Movement."

Having learned many things from 12Stone's previous campus start-ups, the church knew that being much more involved in the process of the new churches and more centralized in leadership would create healthier campuses. When the church launched the second, third, and fourth campuses, they had more of a hands-off approach. As the team applied what they learned from earlier launches and realized that adding five new sites at once would more than double their locations, 12Stone began the process of establishing better communication, better leadership training, and consistent campus feedback even before the new sites launched.

QUINTUPLETS ARE BORN

12Stone successfully launched all five campuses on the same Sunday in January 2015. This unique event was covered by local news, providing even more publicity and adding to the numbers of people who came. The long process of replacing church volunteers was also a success. The "sending pioneers" stepped up and have filled in the gaps. Launching five sites at once was an incredible achievement, but many of the new leaders and volunteers may not have risen to the occasion without the new campuses. In 2016, one of the five new campuses broke ground on a permanent facility, just one year after the launch.

12Stone understood the importance of sending pioneers who would leave their current place of worship and step out to serve at a new campus. In the New

Testament, James—the half-brother of Jesus—stayed back at the Jerusalem church to care for the believers there, while others left Jerusalem as "pioneers" in the field. Timothy cared for the church in Ephesus (1 Tim. 1:3), and Titus, the churches of Crete (Titus 1:5). Paul started upwards of fourteen churches (some believe this number to be much higher), and each was led by one of Paul's apprentice leaders—many who left homes as "pioneers" to spread the gospel to diverse people.

12Stone realized the importance of being missionaries in one's own country of origin—but to a different group of people. If they remained caught up in ministering to people who were similar, many would live their life without hearing about Jesus.

> How then will they call on him in whom they have not believed? And how are they to believe in him of whom they have never heard? And how are they to hear without someone preaching? And how are they to preach unless they are sent? As it is written, "How beautiful are the feet of those who preach the good news!"
>
> – ROMANS 10:14-15 ESV

12Stone knew that they were the "feet of those who preach the good news," and its members understood the benefit of healthy campuses with the same vision and goal: saved lives from hearing the gospel!

QUESTIONS TO CONSIDER

- Are you willing to put in the blood, sweat, and tears that it takes to birth quintuplet churches?

- Are you willing to seek the Lord to see if how you might serve Him, even if it means leaving your current church?

- Are you willing to do something like birth multiple campuses the way God leads?

TAKEAWAY POINTS TO ACT ON:

1. *Multi-site churches require hard work and effective leadership.* Launching multiple sites at one time is usually not done because it is not easy. Just finding five adequate meeting spaces required an army of people looking and investigating. Training leaders and replacing volunteers can be overwhelming to the staff. Don't do a multi-site style of church launch just because another church does it. Seek the Lord's leading for your unique church. Certainly, if your church does not have experience in launching a new campus, you should gain experience in launching single sites first. 12Stone made many adjustments launching the new five because of the three they launched before.

2. *Finding adequate rented meeting space takes time and diligence.* Acquiring multiple locations for the multi-campus launch may be the most daunting task for churches attempting to do so. 12Stone Church started with a list of 400 and still had many challenges. Don't underestimate this aspect of church launching.

3. *This "Pioneer Movement" was only possible because of leadership development.* 12Stone Church has an ongoing church residency program to raise up young men and women for Christian service. The church was able to make this kind of unreasonable expansion happen because the church is already bringing up leaders. Keep training and bringing up leaders. Christ's church needs new leaders every generation.

4. *Everyone was involved.* Some were "going pioneers" and some were "sending pioneers," but everyone had a crucial role. Prepare your church members to be willing to either "go and start-up" or "send and step-up." Make it encouraging and fun. Help everyone see the vision of the church working together to serve each other and spread the gospel.

5. *Consider the stewardship involved.* Launching multiple sites at once can be encouraging and

momentum building for everyone involved. Pastors and leaders can be trained together. Previously inactive members are motivated to volunteer and serve. Investigate whether launching multiple sites might create less financial burden. Sometimes it is good for churches to step back and plan their growth. The best ideas are not always obvious.

6. *Church campuses shouldn't be left to flounder on their own.* Consider whether you need to keep some things centralized after the church launch. Centralized leadership and support requires tremendous communication and leadership. Many start-up churches struggle because they don't have much support. Since 12Stone was giving birth to Quintuplets, they knew from the beginning that these five launches needed intentional support and leadership. Make sure the leaders you bring on the team are willing to work within the support structure.

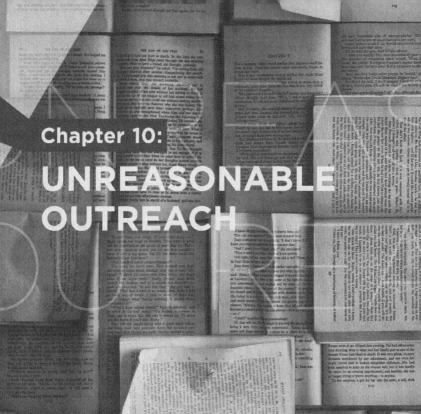

Chapter 10:

UNREASONABLE OUTREACH

AT 90 YEARS old, Eleanor had seen it all. Religion had chewed her up and spit her out many years ago. It was all about obeying the rules and keeping your nose clean. Those who aren't righteous don't deserve pity or compassion, or so she had been told. Like her aged, wrinkled skin, her heart was wrinkled and tired of a God who only made demands. She had heard far too many demands over her long years. She didn't want to hear any more.

But a neighbor, a member of an *unreasonable* church, gave her a free book that presented her with a new perspective. God wasn't just about demands, but God was also about mercy and forgiveness. This book helped her see that the Bible's core message is the gracious gospel of Jesus Christ. How would Eleanor respond?

WORDS OF LIFE

Just a couple of days after Jesus had died and had been buried, two of His followers walked on a dusty road from Jerusalem to Emmaus—sad and despondent over the previous days' events. These two men (and many, many others) had put all of their hopes and dreams into Jesus, believing He was the promised Jewish Messiah!

This was the One, they believed, who would free the Jewish people from Roman oppression and establish God's rule from Jerusalem. But now, their "Messiah" lay in a tomb after being brutally crucified—the most horrible mode of death in the known world at that time.

As they were walking, an unfamiliar man joined them and asked why they were so sad. "Are you the only one visiting Jerusalem who does not know the things that have happened there in these days?" one of the men asked (Luke 24:18). And they told this unknown man everything that had happened:

> "About Jesus of Nazareth," they replied. "He was a prophet, powerful in word and deed before God and all the people. The chief priests and our rulers handed him over to be sentenced to death, and they crucified him; 21 but we had hoped that he was the one who was going to redeem Israel. And what is more, it is the third day since all this took place. In addition, some of our women amazed us. They went to the tomb early this morning but didn't find his body. They came and told us that they had seen a vision of angels, who said he was alive. 24 Then some of our companions went to the tomb and found it just as the women had said, but they did not see Jesus."
>
> – LUKE 24:19–24 NIV

However, there was a twist in the story! This stranger was Jesus, alive and resurrected—only they didn't recognize Him! Jesus responds:

> How foolish you are, and how slow to believe all that the prophets have spoken! Did not the Messiah have to suffer these things and then enter his glory?" *And beginning with Moses and all the Prophets, he explained to them what was said in all the Scriptures concerning himself.*
> – LUKE 24:25B–27, EMPHASIS ADDED

Jesus went back to the Torah, the first five books of the Old Testament, and showed these two sad men all of the places in Scripture they knew that spoke of what would happen to the Messiah when he arrived. He explained that indeed this "Jesus" was the one spoken of in Scripture. It was not until the three men broke bread together over a meal later on that the two realized Jesus had been in their presence. But by the time they did, he vanished.

They turned to each other and said, likely with wide eyes and shaking hands, "Were not our hearts burning within us while he talked with us on the road and opened the Scriptures to us?" (Luke 24:32)

To the elders of the church of Ephesus, Paul the apostle said almost the same thing. He had been teaching the whole narrative of the Bible to the churches he ministered to for three years and declared:

For I have not hesitated to proclaim to you the whole will of God.

– ACTS 20:27 ESV

A CHURCH OF CHURCHES

The Meeting House is a network of churches across Ontario, Canada, started by Craig and Laura Sider in 1986 with a dream to reach people who had given up on church. As a seeker focused church, the network continued to expand with Toronto as its central hub. In the late 1990s, The Meeting House experienced an acceleration of growth. In the last 16 years, the church has grown from 200 to 5,500 attendees each weekend. Expanding the home church network, revamping Sunday services, and changing the church name to The Meeting House fueled this growth.

As part of the Brethren in Christ (BIC) denomination, The Meeting House is a church focused on personal discipleship, but with a passion for Christian evangelism. Influenced by their Anabaptist, Pietist, and Wesleyan heritage, taking the gospel to the lost through innovative church planting matured and grew the church. After founders Craig and Laura Sider moved to Pennsylvania to continue ministry, Bruxy Cavey became teaching pastor and Tim Day became the lead pastor a few years later. During this time, The Meeting House experienced a 35% annual growth rate.

In 2002, the fellowship launched their Hamilton, Ontario site in a school and later in a movie theater.

Seeing the result of that launch, the leadership team made plans for expansion through similar multi-site launches. The development of the home church network was an emphasis on small group discipleship. The small groups were called "Home Churches", and the results of the new launch and the small groups were staggering. The Meeting House began five new sites and 50 more home churches, as well as a central production site, which serves all of the other sites.

In 2007, they became more focused on engaging their community and investing in local and global compassion. The church launched more sites and 64 more home churches as they invested $3.5 million on local and global compassion ministries. The leadership team challenged the church to exit their comfort zones and engage the world with the gospel. As of 2016, The Meeting House has 18 locations, meeting primarily in movie theaters.

THE GOSPEL FOR ALL PEOPLE

Every five years or so, The Meeting House uses major mission goals to inspire people to grow into greater passion and generosity for the lost. In their third wave of setting these lofty goals, they called the mission "Transform." The goal was to invite 100,000 people to consider the message of Jesus over a four-year period. For a church of 5,000, this was a massive undertaking, and the focus of these 100,000 invitations was to be personal interaction. The church was not interested in creating a media campaign conducted on billboards and the Internet. To reach 100,000 with the gospel, they wanted to create gentle points of contact able to transcend the filter of different cultural backgrounds and beliefs.

Before the Transform mission goals came online, Lead Pastor Tim Day had been working through a narrative style Bible. In his pastoral ministry, he noticed that most people encountered the Bible in bits, jumping in and out of portions without context, and they tended to develop a piece-meal theology sorely lacking continuity and depth. He decided to study straight through the Bible, taking the time to understand the narrative in context.

On his third pass reading through the Bible's chronological story, he wrote a detailed explanation of the entire Bible, culminating in the life of Christ. He wanted to write the commentary for his kids, who would cherish their father's many thoughts. As he finished his notes, the project was over 800 pages long, way too long for his kids (or most other people) to read. He also began to translate the entire New Testament, slowing down to pause and consider every verse. After writing an 800-page commentary and translating every verse in the New Testament, Tim wondered if he could distill the meaning of the whole narrative of Scripture down to a short book. As Tim wrestled with summarizing 800 pages, he also wondered if the shorter work could serve as a conversation starter for the Transform mission goal to reach 100,000 people.

Tim decided he needed to narrow the focus of his work, almost like a Cliffs Notes version so that even a seventh grader could understand. His desire for the narrative was that it would be short, clear, gentle, and comprehensive in its approach, so it could be accessible to anyone from any background. The finished work, *God Enters Stage Left*, was around 120 pages long, hitting all of the plot points in the Bible and keeping the whole theme of redemptive history in context. The book was a complete view of God's plan and purpose in the narrative sweep of Scripture.

DOING THE UNREASONABLE: GIVING IT AWAY

Pastor Tim wanted this work to be in as many hands as possible, so The Meeting House leadership had 10,000 copies printed for the church members to give away. The church invited members to donate money toward printing costs if they could, but if not, the church still encouraged everyone to grab a bunch of books and hand them out. By the first weekend, all 10,000 copies were taken. The church scrambled to print another 10,000 copies quickly, and then after those were taken, a third printing was ordered. Between Christmas and Easter, The Meeting House had distributed almost 30,000 copies of *God Enters Stage Left*.

Since the church worked with a publisher that printed the books as a "custom publishing" contract, the church had complete control of the publishing rights.

At the same time, it meant that the church had the full burden of publishing costs. The Meeting House Church members believed in the project so much that they gave generously. After the donations had been counted, the church ended up being able to give away nearly 30,000 books for just 20 cents each. Funds were available for each of the three printings, even though the books were handed out for free. One donor gave $100,000 toward the printing. The entire check went into the church's growth fund to pay for evangelism and church planting.

Just to put this in perspective, 10,000 copies of a book would get it on the New York Times Best Seller List, and The Meeting House distributed nearly three times that in just a few months. Pastor Tim also works with other churches that would like to distribute the books. He helps churches set up the book with a foreword by the pastor and the churches own branding and contact information. In a day with celebrity pastors making top dollar from lucrative book contracts, this selfless outreach is truly unreasonable. Pastor Tim Day and The Meeting House make no profit on the books.

NO CHECK BIG ENOUGH

Pastor Tim was stunned by the response, and especially moved by one of the first stories of a person trusting Christ as a result of the book giveaways. A Muslim man in his thirties had been stumbling around with faith and questions for many years. When he read *God Enters Stage Left,* he said, "This is what makes sense!' He was baptized into Christ following his study through the book's Biblical narrative. Pastor Tim said, "You couldn't have written me a big enough check for that story."

The Indianapolis Colts Bible Study called two weeks into the church book distribution campaign and asked for a shipment of books. The NFL team bible study group was going to study *God Enters Stage Left*. No one associated with The Meeting House could figure out how the team study group even knew about the book.

After 90-year old Eleanor read *God Enters Left Stage*, she cried for hours because of the harsh, legalistic environment she was raised in. Pastor Tim's book highlighted what was wrong with the toxic legalism she had known, and her grief was replaced with joy. She presented an extensive list of family and friends that she wanted to give copies of the book, all of them hurt by the same legalistic teaching.

For the first time, Eleanor and the Muslim man understood truth as they read through that book. There are many other books that are well written and tell the story of the Bible. Why did this particular book change everything for them?

It doesn't matter what book—it matters what is being *taught* in the book. Jesus gave the whole message of the gospel to those two men on the road to Emmaus using nothing but what we know as the Old Testament (the New Testament had not been penned yet ... it was still being played out!). *God Enters Left Stage* did the same thing. And people's lives changed!

The Word of God is powerful and effective, sharper than any double-edged sword. It "penetrates even to divide soul and spirit, joints and marrow; it judges the thoughts and attitudes of the heart" (Hebrews 4:12 NIV). As the two men on the road to Emmaus described, the whole council of God will make hearts burn within people!

QUESTIONS TO CONSIDER

- How are you reaching people like Eleanor?

- Is your church steering clear of teaching the whole council of God, and if so, why?

- What could be a positive outcome of boldly teaching the whole biblical narrative?

TAKEAWAY POINTS TO ACT ON:

1. *Is ministry more important than money?* Let's face it. The Christian book industry is a multi-billion-dollar industry and it's growing. Tim Day decided that people coming to Christ was a much greater payoff than money or notoriety. He believes the time for pastors and churches to make a lot of money from best-selling books is past and it never really did sit well with people. The gospel is free and should be freely given.

2. *Do you have an active point-of-contact tool for your church?* The Meeting House printed 30,000 books because they saw it as a tool to have conversations with people about Jesus. What tools do your church members have in their hands? What can you create or borrow or recycle to make these tools available? Encourage your church leaders and church members to keep looking for opportunities to

serve and engage the lost; to take the gospel of Christ to people in a clear, compassionate, gentle manner.

3. *Use Tim's book as a tool for your ministry.* Why reinvent the wheel? Tim Day is no longer the lead pastor at The Meeting House. He is now involved in leadership with City Movement, a ministry helping business people, parachurch ministries, and churches work together to advance the gospel in their city. Tim is still willing to help churches mobilize distributions of the book. *God Enters Left Stage* is available at Tim Day's Website: www.timday.org/book. You can contact Tim through his website about book printing and outreach.

4. *Do people in your church understand the whole Biblical narrative?* While so many Christian books are in the "self-help" section, it's refreshing to see that Pastor Tim's emphasis is on the entirety of Scripture. As he sought input on his book from many sources, a key response was the difference of his approach. Perhaps church leaders could gain great wisdom in their evangelistic and discipleship efforts by teaching the Bible as a complete redemptive message.

5. *Are you building an organization or making disciples?* Pastor Tim took the time and effort to study, write about, and even translate the Bible. The Meeting House outreach with tens of thousands of books did not happen by organizational leadership but by the dedicated study of Scripture, with an Ezra-like desire to teach God's Word to the world.

6. *Do your church members have a passion for the lost?* A subplot of this story is that The Meeting House members had to have some understanding of the book they were giving away. By encouraging the church members to give away books, they were encouraging church members to read the books, and study Scripture themselves. Discipleship and evangelism come together as the church works toward the Great Commission.

ARE YOU READY?

THE CHURCHES WHOSE stories appear in this book were not afraid to take on challenges. They humbled themselves and allowed brand new believers to be involved in kingdom work. They put aside age, gender, ethnic and cultural gaps; they reexamined current training procedures. They thought like missionaries and built disciples rather than organizations, and they crossed awkward divides between people with different backgrounds. In short, they did whatever was necessary to help people understand God's Word.

The question is, are you willing to do the same? Are you willing to examine the community you live in and the people in your sphere of influence and ask God what He might have you do to make a difference for the kingdom? It may mean doing something irrational, something that to most people sounds crazy and impossible.

But it could also be the most rational and reasonable thing you ever do. Benjamin Franklin said, "The way to see by faith is to shut the eye of reason".

It is this kind of irrational, nonsensical, unreasonable type of faith that will birth an *unreasonable* church.

Are you ready to be unreasonable?

KNOWL

Acknowledgements

ALTHOUGH MY NAME is on the cover of this book it really does take a team to bring it to life. I've been so fortunate to have an incredible team to help me along the way!

My wife, Christine is an amazing gift to me. She provides lots of support and encouragement for all the various things I have on the fly. My amazing kids, Haley and Hunter are the huge part of my motivation in life. I want to leave the church in a better place than I found it for them and their generation.

Beth Colletti is my long suffering partner in all things unSeminary. If you like what happens with the site it's because she keeps us on track. Thanks, Beth!

Each of the church leaders highlighted in this book are my heroes. Thanks for letting us tell your stories!

I've had the honor of serving under three of the most amazing Senior Pastors over the last nearly 20 years. Each of these guys has been an encouragement and guide to me in my development and growth. Bruxy, thanks for pointing people back to Jesus as the center of our faith. Carey, thanks for your encouragement in so many ways over the years! Tim, thanks for always encouraging me to think a bigger thought in leadership.

There is a group of people who have served in some technical roles that have made this book possible. Without the encouragement and guidance of Caleb Breakey this book would just be another idea in a file. I love the interior book design work that Steven Plummer did... it looks so great. I'm honored to have worked with the team at CreateSpace to bring this project into the world... I love how they are making stuff possible that was simply impossible just a few years ago.

Lastly, thanks to you for leading in your church. You've picked a tough and honorable profession. God wants to do huge things through your dreams. I'm excited to hear what unreasonable stuff is brewing in your ministry. Let me know if I can help in any way.

RICH BIRCH
FALL 2016

ABOUT RICH

I'VE BEEN INVOLVED IN CHURCH LEADERSHIP FOR OVER 20 YEARS. EARLY ON I HAD THE PRIVILEGE OF LEADING IN ONE OF THE VERY FIRST MULTISITE CHURCHES IN NORTH AMERICA. I LED THE CHARGE IN HELPING THE MEETING HOUSE IN TORONTO TO BECOME THE LEADING MULTI-SITE CHURCH IN CANADA WITH OVER 4,500 PEOPLE IN 6 LOCATIONS. (TODAY THEY ARE 18 LOCATIONS WITH SOMEWHERE AROUND 6,000 PEOPLE ATTENDING.) IN ADDITION, I SERVED ON THE LEADERSHIP TEAM OF CONNEXUS COMMUNITY CHURCH IN ONTARIO, A NORTH POINT COMMUNITY CHURCH STRATEGIC PARTNER.

FOR SEVEN YEARS I SERVED AS A PART OF THE FOUR-MEMBER LEAD TEAM AT LIQUID CHURCH IN THE MANHATTAN FACING COMMUNITIES OF NEW JERSEY. IN MY TIME WITH THE CHURCH WE GREW FROM 1 CAMPUS TO 6 ... AND OUR ATTENDANCE GREW TO OVER 3,500 PEOPLE. (THAT'S ACTUAL NUMBERS NOT "PASTOR INFLATED NUMBERS!") AT LIQUID I OVERSAW COMMUNICATIONS, WEEKEND SERVICE PROGRAMMING, CAMPUS EXPANSION AND SPECIAL PROJECTS.

I SPEAK AT CONFERENCES LIKE ORANGE, WFX AND VARIOUS REGIONAL MULTISITE CHURCH EVENTS. I'M A FEATURED WRITER ON AUXANO'S VISION ROOM, CHURCHLEADERS.COM AND MINISTRYBRIEFING.

I'M HONORED BLOG AND PODCAST WEEKLY AT UNSEMINARY.COM

I'M MARRIED TO CHRISTINE AND TOGETHER WE PARENT TWO WONDERFUL TEENS, HALEY AND HUNTER. COLLECTIVELY WE TRY TO KEEP OUR DOG, RORY, FROM CHEWING EVERYTHING THAT LANDS ON THE FLOOR.

FEEDBACK

WE WANT TO HEAR WHAT YOU THOUGHT OF
"UNREASONABLE CHURCHES". GIVE US SOME
FEEDBACK SO WE CAN IMPROVE THE NEXT BOOK!

FREE TEAM DISCUSSION PRINTABLES
WHEN YOU LEAVE FEEDBACK AT:
UNSEMINARY.COM/BOOKFEEDBACK

PODCAST

LOVE HEARING THESE STORIES OF UNREASONABLE CHURCHES?

WE SHARE NEW STORIES EVERY WEEK ON OUR PODCAST. WE'D BE HONORED TO HAVE YOU SUBSCRIBE:

UNSEMINARY.COM/ABOUTPODCAST

41607400R00098

Made in the USA
San Bernardino, CA
16 November 2016